The Gospel of
Buddha

The Gospel of
Buddha

CONTENT

The "Gospel of Buddha" is a 19th century compilation from a variety of Buddhist texts by Paul Carus. It is modelled on the New Testament and was very widely read. It was even recommended by Ceylonese Buddhist leaders as a teaching tool for Buddhist children.

Rejoice The Disciple Speaks

REJOICE REJOICE at the glad tidings! The Buddha our Lord has found the root of all evil; he has shown us the way of salvation. The Buddha dispels the illusions of our mind and redeems us from the terror of death.

The Buddha, our Lord, brings comfort to the weary and sorrow-laden; he restores peace to those who are broken down under the burden of life. He gives courage to the weak when they would fain give up self-reliance and hope. You who suffer from the tribulations of life, you who have to struggle and endure, you who yearn for a life of truth, rejoice at the glad tidings! There is balm for the wounded, and there is bread for the hungry. There is water for the thirsty, and there is hope for the despairing. There is light for those in darkness, and there is inexhaustible blessing for the upright.

Heal your wounds, you wounded, and eat your fill, you hungry. Rest, you weary, and you who are thirsty quench your thirst. Look up to the light, you who sit in darkness; be full of good cheer, you who are forlorn.

Trust in truth, You who love the truth, for the kingdom of righteousness is founded upon earth. The darkness of error is dispelled by the light of truth. We can see our way and take firm and certain steps. The Buddha, our Lord, has revealed the truth. The truth cures our diseases and redeems us from perdition; the truth strengthens us in life and in death; the truth alone can conquer the evils of error. Rejoice at the glad tidings!

Samsara And Nirvana

LOOK about and contemplate life! Everything is transient and nothing endures. There is birth and death, growth and decay; there is combination and separation. The glory of the world is like a flower: it stands in full bloom in the morning and fades in the heat of the day.

Wherever you look, there is a rushing and a struggling, and an eager pursuit of pleasure. There is a panic flight from pain and death, and hot are the flames of burning desires. The world is Vanity Fair, full of changes and transformations. All is Samsara, the turning Wheel of Existence.

Is there nothing permanent in the world? Is there, in the universal turmoil no resting-place where our troubled heart can find peace? Is there nothing everlasting? Oh, that we could have cessation of anxiety, that our burning desires would be extinguished! When shall the mind become tranquil and composed?

The Buddha, our Lord, was grieved at the ills of life. He saw the vanity of worldly happiness and sought salvation in the one thing that will not fade or perish, but will abide for ever and ever.

You who long for life, learn that immortality is hidden in transiency. You who wish for happiness without the sting of regret, lead a life of righteousness. You who yearn for riches, receive treasures that are eternal. Truth is wealth, and a life of truth is happiness.

All compounds will be dissolved again, but the verities which determine all combinations and separations as laws of nature endure for ever and aye. Bodies fall to dust, but the truths of the mind will not be destroyed.

Truth knows neither birth nor death; it has no beginning and no end. Welcome the truth. The truth is the immortal part of the mind. Establish the truth in your mind, for the truth is the image of the eternal; it portrays the immutable; it reveals the everlasting; the truth gives unto mortals the boon of immortality.

The Buddha has proclaimed the truth; let the truth of the Buddha dwell in your hearts. Extinguish in yourselves every desire that antagonises the Buddha, and in the perfection of your spiritual growth you will become like unto him. That of your heart which cannot or will not develop into Buddha must perish, for it is mere illusion and unreal; it is the source of your error; it is the cause of your misery.

You attain to immortality by filling your minds with truth. Therefore, become like unto vessels fit to receive the Master's words. Cleanse yourselves of evil and sanctify your lives. There is no other way of reaching truth.

Learn to distinguish between Self and Truth. Self is the cause of selfishness and the source of evil; truth cleaves to no self; it is universal and leads to justice and righteousness. Self, that which seems to those who love their self as their being, is not the eternal, the everlasting, the imperishable. Seek not self, but seek the truth.

If we liberate our souls from our petty selves, wish no ill to others, and become clear as a crystal diamond reflecting the light of truth, what a radiant picture will appear in us mirroring things as they are, without the admixture of burning desires, without the distortion of erroneous illusion, without the agitation of clinging and unrest.

Yet you love self and will not abandon self-love. So be it, but then, verily, you should learn to distinguish between the false self and the true self. The ego with all its egotism is the false self. It is an unreal illusion and a perishable combination. He only who identifies his self with the truth will attain Nirvana; and he who has entered Nirvana has attained Buddhahood; he has acquired the highest good; he has become eternal and immortal.

All compound things shall be dissolved again, worlds will break to pieces and our individualities will be scattered; but the words of Buddha will remain for ever.

The extinction of self is salvation; the annihilation of self is the condition of enlightenment; the blotting out of self is Nirvana.

Happy is he who has ceased to live for pleasure and rests in the truth. Verily his composure and tranquillity of mind are the highest bliss.

Let us take our refuge in the Buddha, for he has found the everlasting in the transient. Let us take our refuge in that which is the immutable in the changes of existence. Let us take our refuge in the truth that is established through the enlightenment of the Buddha. Let us take our refuge in the community of those who seek the truth and endeavour to live in the truth.

Truth, The Saviour

THE things of the world and its inhabitants are subject to change. They are combinations of elements that existed before, and all living creatures are what their past actions made them; for the law of cause and effect is uniform and without exception.

But in the changing things there is a constancy of law, and when the law is seen there is truth. The truth lies hidden in Samsara as the permanent in its changes.

Truth desires to appear; truth longs to become conscious; truth strives to know itself.

There is truth in the stone, for the stone is here; and no power in the world, no god, no man, no demon, can destroy its existence. But the stone has no consciousness. There is truth in the plant and its life can expand; the plant grows and blossoms and bears fruit. Its beauty is marvellous, but it has no consciousness. There is truth in the animal; it moves about and perceives its surroundings; it distinguishes and learns to choose. There is consciousness, but it is not yet the consciousness of Truth. It is a consciousness of self only.

The consciousness of self dims the eyes of the mind and hides the truth. It is the origin of error, it is the source of illusion, it is the germ of evil. Self begets selfishness. There is no evil but what flows from self. There is no wrong but what is done by the assertion of self. Self is the beginning of all hatred, of iniquity and slander, of impudence and indecency, of theft and robbery, of oppression and bloodshed. Self is Mara, the tempter, the evil-doer, the creator of mischief. Self entices with pleasures. Self promises a fairy's paradise. Self is the veil of Maya, the enchanter. But the pleasures of self are unreal, its paradisian labyrinth is the road to misery, and its fading beauty kindles the flames of desires that never can be satisfied.

Who shall deliver us from the power of self? Who shall save us from misery? Who shall restore us to a life of blessedness?

There is misery in the world of Samsara; there is much misery and pain. But greater than all the misery is the bliss of truth. Truth gives peace to the yearning mind; it conquers error; it quenches the flames of desires; it leads to Nirvana. Blessed is he who has found the peace of Nirvana. He is at rest in the struggles and tribulations of life; he is above all changes; he is above birth and death; he remains unaffected by the evils of life.

Blessed is he who has found enlightenment. He conquers, although he may be wounded; he is glorious and happy, although he may suffer; he is strong, although he may break down under the burden of his work; he is immortal, although he will die. The essence of his being is purity and goodness.

Blessed is he who has attained the sacred state of Buddhahood, for he is fit to work out the salvation of his fellow beings. The truth has taken its abode in him. Perfect wisdom illumines his understanding, and righteousness ensouls the purpose of all his actions. The truth is a living power for good, indestructible and invincible! Work the truth out in your mind, and spread it among mankind, for truth alone is the saviour from evil and misery. The Buddha has found the truth and the truth has been proclaimed by the Buddha! Blessed be the Buddha!

The Enlightenment

THERE was in Kapilavatthu a Sakya king, strong of purpose and reverenced by all men, a descendant of the Okkakas, who call themselves Gotama, and his name was Suddhodana or Pure-Rice. His wife Mayadevi was beautiful as the water-lily and pure in mind as the lotus. As the Queen of Heaven, she lived on earth, untainted by desire, and immaculate.

The king, her husband, honoured her in her holiness, and the spirit of truth, glorious and strong in his wisdom like unto a white elephant, descended upon her. When she knew that the hour of motherhood was near, she asked the king to send her home to her parents; and Suddhodana, anxious about his wife and the child she would bear him, willingly granted her request.

At Lumbini there is a beautiful grove, and when Mayadevi passed through it the trees were one mass of fragrant flowers and many birds were warbling in their branches. The Queen, wishing to stroll through the shady walks, left her golden palanquin, and, when she reached the giant sala tree in the midst of the grove, felt that her hour had come. She took hold of a branch. Her attendants hung a curtain about her and retired. When the pain of travail came upon her, four pure-minded angels of the great Brahma held out a golden net to receive the babe, who came forth from her right side like the rising sun bright and perfect.

The Brahma-angels took the child and placing him before the mother said "Rejoice, O queen, a mighty son has been born unto thee."

At her couch stood an aged woman imploring the heavens to bless the child. All the worlds were flooded with light. The blind received their sight by longing to see the coming glory of the Lord; the deaf and dumb spoke with one another of the good omens indicating the birth of the Buddha to be. The crooked became straight; the lame walked. All prisoners were freed from their chains and the fires of all the hells were extinguished.

No clouds gathered in the skies and the polluted streams became clear, whilst celestial music rang through the air and the angels rejoiced with gladness. With no selfish or partial joy but for the sake of the law they rejoiced, for creation engulfed in the ocean of pain was now to obtain release. The cries of beasts were hushed; all malevolent beings received a loving heart, and peace reigned on earth. Mara, the evil one, alone was grieved and rejoiced not.

The Naga kings, earnestly desiring to show their reverence for most excellent law, as they had paid honour to former Buddhas, now went to greet the Bodhisattva. They scattered before him mandara flowers, rejoicing with heartfelt joy to pay their religious homage.

The royal father, pondering the meaning of these signs, was now full of joy and now sore distressed. The queen mother, beholding her child and the commotion which his birth created, felt in her timorous heart the pangs of doubt.

Now there was at that time in a grove near Lumbini Asita, a rishi, leading the life of a hermit. He was a Brahman of dignified mien, famed not only for wisdom and scholarship, but also for his skill in the interpretation of signs. And the king invited him to see the royal babe.

The seer, beholding the prince, wept and sighed deeply. And when the king saw the tears of Asita he became alarmed and asked: "Why has the sight of my son caused thee grief and pain?"

But Asita's heart rejoiced, and, knowing the king's mind to be perplexed, he addressed him, saying: "The king, like the moon when full, should feel great joy, for he has begotten a wondrously noble son. I do not worship Brahma, but I worship this child; and the gods in the temples will descend from their places of honour to adore him. Banish all anxiety and doubt. The spiritual omens manifested indicate that the child now born will bring deliverance to the whole world.

"Recollecting that I myself am old, on that account I could not hold my tears; for now my end is coming on and I shall not see the glory of this babe. For this son of thine will rule the world. The wheel of empire will come to him. He will either be a king of kings to govern all the lands of the earth, or verily will become a Buddha.

He is born for the sake of everything that lives. His pure teaching will be like the shore that receives the shipwrecked. His power of meditation will be like a cool lake; and all creatures parched with the drought of lust may freely drink thereof. On the fire of covetousness he will cause the cloud of his mercy to rise, so that the rain of the law may extinguish it. The heavy gates of despondency will he open, and give deliverance to all creatures ensnared in the self-entwined meshes of folly and ignorance. The king of the law has come forth to rescue from bondage all the poor, the miserable, the helpless."

When the royal parents heard Asita's words they rejoiced in their hearts and named their new-born infant Siddhattha, that is he who has accomplished his purpose.

And the queen said to her sister, Pajapati: "A mother who has borne a future Buddha will never give birth to another child. I shall soon leave this world, my husband, the king, and Siddhattha, my child. When I am gone, be thou a mother to him." And Pajapati wept and promised.

When the queen had departed from the living, Pajapati took the boy Siddhattha and reared him. And as the light of the moon increases little by little, so the royal child grew from day to day in mind and in body; and truthfulness and love resided in his heart. When a year had passed Suddhodana the king made Pajapati his queen and there was never a better stepmother than she.

The Ties Of Life

WHEN Siddhattha had grown to youth, his father desired to see him married, and he sent to all his kinsfolk, commanding them to bring their princesses that the prince might select one of them as his wife.

But the kinsfolk replied and said: "The prince is young and delicate; nor has he learned any of the sciences. He would not be able to maintain our daughter, and should there be war he would be unable to cope with the enemy."

The prince was not boisterous, but pensive in his nature. He loved to stay under the great jambu-tree in the garden of his father, and, observing the ways of the world, gave himself up to meditation. And the prince said to his father: "Invite our kinsfolk that they may see me and put my strength to the test." And his father did as his son bade him.

When the kinsfolk came, and the people of the city Kapilavatthu had assembled to test the prowess and scholarship of the prince, he proved himself manly in all the exercises both of the body and of the mind, and there was no rival among the youths and men of India who could surpass him in any test, bodily or mental. He replied to all the questions of the sages; but when he questioned them, even the wisest among them were silenced.

Then Siddhattha chose himself a wife. He selected his cousin Yasodhara, the gentle daughter of the king of Koli. In their wedlock was born a son whom they named Rahula which means "fetter" or "tie," and King Suddhodana, glad that an heir was born to his son, said: "The prince having begotten a son, will love him as I love the prince. This will be a strong tie to bind Siddhattha's heart to the interests of the world, and the kingdom of the Sakyas will remain under the sceptre of my descendants."

With no selfish aim, but regarding his child and the people at large, Siddhattha, the prince, attended to his religious duties, bathing his body in the holy Ganges and cleansing his heart in the waters of the law. Even as men desire to give happiness to their children, so did he long to give peace to the world.

The Three Woes

THE palace which the king had given to the prince was resplendent with all the luxuries of India; for the king was anxious to see his son happy. All sorrowful sights, all misery, and all knowledge of misery were kept away from Siddhattha, for the king desired that no troubles should come nigh him; he should not know that there was evil in the world.

But as the chained elephant longs for the wilds of the jungles, so the prince was eager to see the world, and he asked his father, the king, for permission to do so. And Suddhodana ordered a jewel-fronted chariot with four stately horses to be held ready, and commanded the roads to be adorned where his son would pass.

The houses of the city were decorated with curtains and banners, and spectators arranged themselves on either side, eagerly gazing at the heir to the throne. Thus Siddhattha rode with Channa, his charioteer, through the streets of the city, and into a country watered by rivulets and covered with pleasant trees.

There by the wayside they met an old man with bent frame, wrinkled face and sorrowful brow, and the prince asked the charioteer: "Who is this? His head is white, his eyes are bleared, and his body is withered. He can barely support himself on his staff."

The charioteer, much embarrassed, hardly dared speak the truth. He said: "These are the symptoms of old age. This same man was once a suckling child, and as a youth full of sportive life; but now, as years have passed away, his beauty is gone and the strength of his life is wasted."

Siddhattha was greatly affected by the words of the charioteer, and he sighed because of the pain of old age. "What joy or pleasure can men take," he thought to himself, "when they know they must soon wither and pine away!"

And lo! while they were passing on, a sick man appeared on the way-side, gasping for breath, his body disfigured, convulsed and groaning with pain. The prince asked his charioteer: "What kind of man is this?" And the charioteer replied and said: "This man is sick. The four elements of his body are confused and out of order. We are all subject to such conditions: the poor and the rich, the ignorant and the wise, all creatures that have bodies are liable to the same calamity."

And Siddhattha was still more moved. All pleasures appeared stale to him, and he loathed the joys of life.

The charioteer sped the horses on to escape the dreary sight, when suddenly they were stopped in their fiery course. Four persons passed by, carrying a corpse; and the prince, shuddering at the sight of a lifeless body, asked the charioteer: "What is this they carry? There are streamers and flower garlands; but the men that follow are overwhelmed with grief!"

The charioteer replied: "This is a dead man: his body is stark; his life is gone; his thoughts are still; his family and the friends who loved him now carry the corpse to the grave." And the prince was full of awe and terror: "Is this the only dead man," he asked, "or does the world contain other instances?"

With a heavy heart the charioteer replied: "All over the world it is the same. He who begins life must end it. There is no escape from death."

With bated breath and stammering accents the prince exclaimed: "O worldly men! How fatal is your delusion! Inevitably your body will crumble to dust, yet carelessly, unheedingly, ye live on." The charioteer observing the deep impression these sad sights had made on the prince, turned his horses and drove back to the city.

When they passed by the palace of the nobility, Kisa Gotami, a young princess and niece of the king, saw Siddhattha in his manliness and beauty, and, observing the thoughtfulness of his countenance, said: "Happy the father that begot thee, happy the mother that nursed thee, happy the wife that calls husband this lord so glorious."

The prince hearing this greeting, said: "Happy are they that have found deliverance. Longing for peace of mind, I shall seek the bliss of Nirvana."

Then asked Kisa Gotami: "How is Nirvana attained?" The prince paused, and to him whose mind was estranged from wrong the answer came: "When the fire of lust is gone out, then Nirvana is gained; when the fires of hatred and delusion are gone out, then Nirvana is gained; when the troubles of mind, arising from blind credulity, and all other evils have ceased, then Nirvana is gained!"

Siddhattha handed her his precious pearl necklace as a reward for the wisdom she had inspired in him, and having returned home looked with disdain upon the treasures of his palace.

His wife welcomed him and entreated him to tell her the cause of his grief. He said: "I see everywhere the impression of change; therefore, my heart is heavy. Men grow old, sicken, and die. That is enough to take away the zest of life."

The king, his father, hearing that the prince had become estranged from pleasure, was greatly overcome with sorrow and like a sword it pierced his heart.

The Bodhisattvas Renunciation

IT was night. The prince found no rest on his soft pillow; he arose and went out into the garden. "Alas!" he cried "all the world is full of darkness and ignorance; there is no one who knows how to cure the ills of existence." And he groaned with pain.

Siddhattha sat down beneath the great jambu-tree and gave himself to thought, pondering on life and death and the evils of decay. Concentrating his mind he became free from confusion. All low desires vanished from his heart and perfect tranquillity came over him.

In this state of ecstasy he saw with his mental eye all the misery and sorrow of the world; he saw the pains of pleasure and the inevitable certainty of death that hovers over every being; yet men are not awakened to the truth. And a deep compassion seized his heart.

While the prince was pondering on the problem of evil, he beheld with his mind's eye under the jambu tree a lofty figure endowed with majesty, calm and dignified. "Whence comest thou, and who mayst thou be" asked the prince.

In reply the vision said: "I am a samana. Troubled at the thought of old age, disease, and death I have left my home to seek the path of salvation. All things hasten to decay; only the truth abideth forever. Everything changes, and there is no permanency;

yet the words of the Buddhas are immutable. I long for the happiness that does not decay; the treasure that will never perish; the life that knows of no beginning and no end. Therefore, I have destroyed all worldly thought. I have retired into an unfrequented dell to live in solitude; and, begging for food, I devote myself to the one thing needful."

Siddhattha asked: "Can peace be gained in this world of unrest? I am struck with the emptiness of pleasure and have become disgusted with lust. All oppresses me, and existence itself seems intolerable."

The samana replied: "Where heat is, there is also a possibility of cold; creatures subject to pain possess the faculty of pleasure; the origin of evil indicates that good can be developed. For these things are correlatives. Thus where there is much suffering, there will be much bliss, if thou but open thine eyes to behold it. Just as a man who has fallen into a heap of filth ought to seek the great pond of water covered with lotuses, which is near by: even so seek thou for the great deathless lake of Nirvana to wash off the defilement of wrong. If the lake is not sought, it is not the fault of the lake. Even so when there is a blessed road leading the man held fast by wrong to the salvation of Nirvana, if the road is not walked upon, it is not the fault of the road, but of the person. And when a man who is oppressed with sickness, there being a physician who can heal him, does not avail himself of the physician's help, that is not the fault of the physician. Even so when a man oppressed by the malady of wrong-doing does not seek the spiritual guide of enlightenment, that is no fault of the evil-destroying guide."

The prince listened to the noble words of his visitor and said: "Thou bringest good tidings, for now I know that my purpose will be accomplished. My father advises me to enjoy life and to undertake worldly duties, such as will bring honour to me and to our house. He tells me that I am too young still, that my pulse beats too full to lead a religious life."

The venerable figure shook his head and replied: "Thou shouldst know that for seeking a religious life no time can be inopportune."

A thrill of joy passed through Siddhattha's heart. "Now is the time to seek religion," he said; "now is the time to sever all ties that would prevent me from attaining perfect enlightenment; now is the time to wander into homelessness and, leading a mendicant's life, to find the path of deliverance."

The celestial messenger heard the resolution of Siddhattha with approval. "Now, indeed" he added, "is the time to seek religion. Go, Siddhattha, and accomplish thy purpose. For thou art Bodhisatta, the Buddha-elect; thou art destined to enlighten the world. Thou art the Tathagata, the great master, for thou wilt fulfil all righteousness and be Dharmaraja, the king of truth. Thou art Bhagavat, the Blessed One, for thou art called upon to become the saviour and redeemer of the world. Fulfil thou the perfection of truth. Though the thunderbolt descend upon thy head, yield thou never to the allurements that beguile men from the path of truth. As the sun at all seasons pursues his own course, nor ever goes on another, even so if thou forsake not the straight path of righteousness, thou shalt become a Buddha. Persevere in thy quest and thou shalt find what thou seekest. Pursue thy aim unswervingly and thou shalt gain the prize. Struggle earnestly and thou shalt conquer. The benediction of all deities, of all saints of all that seek light is upon thee, and heavenly wisdom guides thy steps. Thou shalt be the Buddha, our Master, and our Lord; thou shalt enlighten the world and save mankind from perdition."

Having thus spoken, the vision vanished, and Siddhattha's heart was filled with peace. He said to himself: "I have awakened to the truth and I am resolved to accomplish my purpose. I will sever all the ties that bind me to the world, and I will go out from my home to seek the way of salvation. The Buddhas are beings whose words cannot fail: there is no departure from truth in their speech.

For as the fall of a stone thrown into the air, as the death of a mortal, as the sunrise at dawn, as the lion's roar when he leaves his lair, as the delivery of a woman with child, as all these things are sure and certain-even so the word of the Buddhas is sure and cannot fail. Verily I shall become a Buddha."

The prince returned to the bedroom of his wife to take a last farewell glance at those whom he dearly loved above all the treasures of the earth. He longed to take the infant once more into his arms and kiss him with a parting kiss. But the child lay in the arms of his mother, and the prince could not lift him without awakening both. There Siddhattha stood gazing at his beautiful wife and his beloved son, and his heart grieved. The pain of parting overcame him powerfully. Although his mind was determined, so that nothing, be it good or evil, could shake his resolution, the tears flowed freely from his eyes, and it was beyond his power to check their stream. But the prince tore himself away with a manly heart, suppressing his feelings but not extinguishing his memory.

The Bodhisattva mounted his noble steed Kanthaka, and when he left the palace, Mara stood in the gate and stopped him: "Depart not, O my Lord," exclaimed Mara. "In seven days from now the wheel of empire will appear, and will make thee sovereign over the four continents and the two thousand adjacent islands. Therefore, stay, my Lord."

The Bodhisattva replied: "Well do I know that the wheel of empire will appear to me; but it is not sovereignty that I desire. I will become a Buddha and make all the world shout for joy."

Thus Siddhattha, the prince, renounced power and worldly pleasures, gave up his kingdom, severed all ties, and went into homelessness. He rode out into the silent night, accompanied only by his faithful charioteer Channa. Darkness lay upon the earth, but the stars shone brightly in the heavens.

King Bimbisara

SIDDHATTHA had cut his waving hair and had exchanged his royal robe for a mean dress of the colour of the ground. Having sent home Channa, the charioteer, together with the noble steed Kanthaka, to King Suddhodana to bear him the message that the prince had left the world, the Bodhisattva walked along on the highroad with a beggar's bowl in his hand.

Yet the majesty of his mind was ill-concealed under the poverty of his appearance. His erect gait betrayed his royal birth and his eyes beamed with a fervid zeal for truth. The beauty of his youth was transfigured by holiness and surrounded his head like a halo. All the people who saw this unusual sight gazed at him in wonder. Those who were in haste arrested their steps and looked back; and there was no one who did not pay him homage.

Having entered the city of Rajagaha, the prince went from house to house silently waiting till the people offered him food. Wherever the Blessed One came, the people gave him what they had; they bowed before him in humility and were filled with gratitude because he condescended to approach their homes. Old and young people were moved and said: "This is a noble muni! His approach is bliss. What a great joy for us!"

And King Bimbisara, noticing the commotion in the city, inquired the cause of it, and when he learned the news sent one of his attendants to observe the stranger. Having heard that the muni must be a Sakya and of noble family, and that he had retired to the bank of a flowing river in the woods to eat the food in his bowl, the king was moved in his heart; he donned his royal robe, placed his golden crown upon his head and went out in the company of aged and wise counsellors to meet his mysterious guest.

The king found the muni of the Sakya race seated under a tree. Contemplating the composure of his face and the gentleness of his deportment, Bimbisara greeted him reverently and said: "O samana, thy hands are fit to grasp the reins of an empire and should not hold a beggar's bowl. I am sorry to see thee wasting thy youth. Believing that thou art of royal descent, I invite thee to join me in the government of my country and share my royal power. Desire for power is becoming to the noble-minded, and wealth should not be despised. To grow rich and lose religion is not true gain. But he who possesses all three, power, wealth, and religion, enjoying them in discretion and with wisdom, him I call a great master."

The great Sakyamuni lifted his eyes and replied: "Thou art known, O king, to be liberal and religious, and thy words are prudent. A kind man who makes good use of wealth is rightly said to possess a great treasure; but the miser who hoards up his riches will have no profit. Charity is rich in returns; charity is the greatest wealth, for though it scatters, it brings no repentance."

"I have severed all ties because I seek deliverance. How is it possible for me to return to the world? He who seeks religious truth, which is the highest treasure of all, must leave behind all that can concern him or draw away his attention, and must be bent upon that one goal alone. He must free his soul from covetousness and lust, and also from the desire for power."

"Indulge in lust but a little, and lust like a child will grow. Wield worldly power and you will be burdened with cares. Better than sovereignty over the earth, better than living in heaven, better than lordship over all the worlds, is the fruit of holiness. The Bodhisattva has recognised the illusory nature of wealth and will not take poison as food. Will a fish that has been baited still covet the hook, or an escaped bird love the net? Would a rabbit rescued from the serpent's mouth go back to be devoured? Would a man who has burnt his hand with a torch take up the torch after he had dropped it to the earth? Would a blind man who has recovered his sight desire to spoil his eyes again?"

"The sick man suffering from fever seeks for a cooling medicine. Shall we advise him to drink that which will increase the fever? Shall we quench a fire by heaping fuel upon it?"

"I pray thee, pity me not. Rather pity those who are burdened with the cares of royalty and the worry of great riches. They enjoy them in fear and trembling, for they are constantly threatened with a loss of those boons on whose possession their hearts are set, and when they die they cannot take along either their gold or the kingly diadem."

"My heart hankers after no vulgar profit, so I have put away my royal inheritance and prefer to be free from the burdens of life. Therefore, try not to entangle me in new relationships and duties, nor hinder me from completing the work I have begun. I regret to leave thee. But I will go to the sages who can teach me religion and so find the path on which we can escape evil."

"May thy country enjoy peace and prosperity, and may wisdom be shed upon thy rule like the brightness of the noon-day sun. May thy royal power be strong and may righteousness be the sceptre in thine hand."

The king, clasping his hands with reverence, bowed down before Sakyamuni and said: "Mayest thou obtain that which thou seekest, and when thou hast obtained it, come back, I pray thee, and receive me as thy disciple." The Bodhisattva parted from the king in friendship and goodwill, and purposed in his heart to grant his request.

The Bodhisattva's Search

ALARA and Uddaka were renowned as teachers among the Brahmans, and there was no one in those days who surpassed them in learning and philosophical knowledge. The Bodhisattva went to them and sat at their feet. He listened to their doctrines of the atman or self, which is the ego of the mind and the doer of all doings. He learned their views of the transmigration of souls and of the law of karma; how the souls of bad men had to suffer by being reborn in men of low caste, in animals, or in hell, while those who purified themselves by libation, by sacrifices, and by self-mortification would become kings, or Brahmans, or devas, so as to rise higher and higher in the grades of existence. He studied their incantations and offerings and the methods by which they attained deliverance of the ego from material existence in states of ecstasy.

Alara said: "What is that self which perceives the actions of the five roots of mind, touch, smell, taste, sight, and hearing? What is that which is active in the two ways of motion, in the hands and in the feet? The problem of the soul appears in the expressions 'I say,' 'I know and perceive,' 'I come,' and 'I go' or 'I will stay here.' Thy soul is not thy body; it is not thy eye, not thy ear, not thy nose, not thy tongue, nor is it thy mind. The I is the one who feels the touch in thy body. The I is the smeller in the nose, the taster in the tongue, the seer in the eye, the hearer in the ear, and the thinker in the mind. The I moves thy hands and thy feet. The I is thy soul. Doubt in the existence of the soul is irreligious, and without discerning this truth there is no way of salvation. Deep speculation will easily involve the mind; it leads to confusion and unbelief; but a purification of the soul leads to the way of escape. True deliverance is reached by removing from the crowd and leading a hermit's life, depending entirely on alms for food. Putting away all desire and clearly recognising the non-existence of matter, we reach a state of perfect emptiness. Here we find the condition of immaterial life. As the munja grass when freed from its horny case, as a sword when drawn from its scabbard, or as the wild bird escaped from its prison, so the ego liberating itself from all limitations, finds perfect release. This is true deliverance, but those only who will have deep faith will learn."

The Bodhisattva found no satisfaction in these teachings. He replied: "People are in bondage, because they have not yet removed the idea of the ego. The thing and its quality are different in our thought, but not in reality. Heat is different from fire in our thought, but you cannot remove heat from fire in reality. You say that you can remove the qualities and leave the thing, but if you think your theory to the end, you will find that this is not so.

"Is not man an organism of many aggregates? Are we not composed of various attributes? Man consists of the material form, of sensation, of thought, of dispositions, and, lastly, of understanding. That which men call the ego when they say 'I am' is not an entity behind the attributes; it originates by their co-operation. There is mind; there is sensation and thought, and there is truth; and truth is mind when it walks in the path of righteousness. But there is no separate ego-soul outside or behind the thought of man. He who believes the ego is a distinct being has no correct conception. The very search for the atman is wrong; it is a wrong start and it will lead you in a false direction."

"How much confusion of thought comes from our interest in self, and from our vanity when thinking 'I am so great,' or 'I have done this wonderful deed?' The thought of thine ego stands between thy rational nature and truth; banish it, and then wilt thou see things as they are. He who thinks correctly will rid himself of ignorance and acquire wisdom. The ideas 'I am' and 'I shall be' or 'I shall not be' do not occur to a clear thinker."

"Moreover, if our ego remains, how can we attain true deliverance? If the ego is to be reborn in any of the three worlds, be it in hell, upon earth, or be it even in heaven, we shall meet again and again the same inevitable doom of sorrow. We shall remain chained to the wheel of individuality and shall be implicated in egotism and wrong. All combination is subject to separation, and we cannot escape birth, disease, old age, and death. Is this a final escape?"

Said Uddaka: "Consider the unity of things. Things are not their parts, yet they exist. The members and organs of thy body are not thine ego, but thine ego possesses all these parts. What, for instance, is the Ganges? Is the sand the Ganges? Is the water the Ganges? Is the hither bank the Ganges? Is the farther bank the Ganges? The Ganges is a mighty river and it possesses all these several qualities. Exactly so is our ego."

But the Bodhisattva replied: "Not so, sir! If we remove the water, the sand, the hither bank and the farther bank where can we find any Ganges? In the same way I observe the activities of man in their harmonious union, but there is no ground for an ego outside its parts."

The Brahman sage, however, insisted on the existence of the ego, saying: "The ego is the doer of our deeds. How can there be karma without a self as its performer? Do we not see around us the effects of karma? What makes men different in character, station, possessions, and fate? It is their karma, and karma includes merit and demerit. The transmigration of the soul is subject to its karma. We inherit from former existences the evil effects of our evil deeds and the good effects of our good deeds. If that were not so, how could we be different?"

The Tathagata meditated deeply on the problems of transmigration and karma, and found the truth that lies in them. "The doctrine of karma," he said, "is undeniable, but the theory of the ego has no foundation. Like everything else in nature, the life of man is subject to the law of cause and effect. The present reaps what the past has sown, and the future is the product of the present. But there is no evidence of the existence of an immutable ego-being, of a self which remains the same and migrates from body to body. There is rebirth but no transmigration."

"Is not this individuality of mine a combination, material as well as mental? Is it not made up of qualities that sprang into being by a gradual evolution? The five roots of sense perception in this organism have come from ancestors who performed these functions. The ideas which I think, came to me partly from others who thought them, and partly they rise from combinations of the ideas in my own mind. Those who have used the same sense-organs, and have thought the same ideas before I was composed into this individuality of mine, are my previous existences; they are my ancestors as much as the I of yesterday is the father of the I of today, and the karma of my past deeds affects the fate of my present existence."

"Supposing there were an atman that performs the actions of the senses then if the door of sight were torn down and the eye plucked out, that atman would be able to peep through the larger aperture and see the forms of its surroundings better and more clearly than before. It would be able to hear sounds better if the ears were torn away; smell better if the nose were cut off; taste better if the tongue were pulled out; and feel better if the body were destroyed."

"I observe the preservation and transmission of character; I perceive the truth of karma, but see no atman whom your doctrine makes the doer of your deeds. There is rebirth without the transmigration of a self. For this atman, this self, this ego in the 'I say' and in the 'I will' is an illusion. If this self were a reality, how could there be an escape from selfhood? The terror of hell would be infinite, and no release could be granted. The evils of existence would not be due to our ignorance and wrong-doing, but would constitute the very nature of our being."

Then the Bodhisattva went to the priests officiating in the temples. But the gentle mind of the Sakyamuni was offended at the unnecessary cruelty performed on the altars of the gods. He said: "Ignorance only can make these men prepare festivals and hold vast meetings for sacrifices. Far better to revere the truth than try to appease the gods by shedding blood. What love can a man possess who believes that the destruction of life will atone for evil deeds? Can a new wrong expiate old wrongs? And can the slaughter of an innocent victim blot out the evil deeds of mankind? This is practicing religion by the neglect of moral conduct. Purify your hearts and cease to kill; that is true religion. Rituals have no efficacy; prayers are vain repetitions; and incantations have no saving power. But to abandon covetousness and lust, to become free from evil passions, and to give up all hatred and ill-will, that is the right sacrifice and the true worship."

Uruvela, Place Of Mortification

THE Bodhisattva went in search of a better system and came to a settlement of five bhikkhus in the jungle of Uruvela; and when the Blessed One saw the life of those five men, virtuously keeping in check their senses, subduing their passions, and practicing austere self-discipline, he admired their earnestness and joined their company. With holy zeal and a strong heart, the Sakyamuni gave himself up to meditative thought and a rigorous mortification of the body. Whereas the five bhikkhus were severe, the Sakyamuni was severer still, and so they revered him, their junior, as their master.

So the Bodhisattva continued for six years patiently torturing himself and suppressing the wants of nature. He trained his body and exercised his mind in the modes of the most rigorous ascetic life. At last, he ate each day one hemp grain only, seeking to cross the ocean of birth and death and to arrive at the shore of deliverance.

And when the Bodhisattva was ahungered, lo! Mara, the Evil One, approached him and said: "Thou art emaciated from fasts, and death is near. What good is thy exertion? Deign to live, and thou wilt be able to do good work." But the Sakyamuni made reply: "O thou friend of the indolent, thou wicked one; for what purpose hast thou come? Let the flesh waste away, if but the mind becomes more tranquil and attention more steadfast. What is life in this world? Death in battle is better to me than that I should live defeated."

And Mara withdrew, saying: "For seven years I have followed the Blessed One step by step, but I have found no fault in the Tathagata."

The Bodhisattva was shrunken and attenuated, and his body was like a withered branch; but the fame of his holiness spread in the surrounding countries, and people came from great distances to see him and receive his blessing. However, the Holy One was not satisfied. Seeking true wisdom he did not find it, and he came to the conclusion that mortification would not extinguish desire nor afford enlightenment in ecstatic contemplation.

Seated beneath a jambu-tree, he considered the state of his mind and the fruits of his mortification. His body had become weaker, nor had his fasts advanced him in his search for salvation, and therefore when he saw that it was not the right path, he proposed to abandon it. He went to bathe in the Neranjara River, but when he strove to leave the water he could not rise on account of his weakness. Then espying the branch of a tree and taking hold of it, he raised himself and left the stream. But while returning to his abode, he staggered and lay as though dead.

There was a chief herdsman living near the grove whose eldest daughter was called Nanda; and Nanda happened to pass by the spot where the Blessed One had swooned, and bowing down before him she offered him rice-milk and he accepted the gift. When he had partaken of the rice-milk all his limbs were refreshed, his mind became clear again, and he was strong to receive the highest enlightenment.

After this occurrence, the Bodhisattva again took some food. His disciples, having witnessed the scene of Nanda and observing the change in his mode of living, were filled with suspicion. They feared that Siddhattha's religious zeal was flagging and that he whom they had hitherto revered as their Master had become oblivious of his high purpose.

When the Bodhisattva saw the bhikkhus turning away from him, he felt sorry for their lack of confidence, and was aware of the loneliness of his life. Suppressing his grief he wandered on alone, and his disciples said, "Siddhattha leaves us to seek a more pleasant abode."

Mara, The Evil One

THE Holy One directed his steps to that blessed Bodhitree beneath whose shade he was to accomplish his search. As he walked, the earth shook and a brilliant light transfigured the world. When he sat down the heavens resounded with joy and all living beings were filled with good cheer. Mara alone, lord of the five desires, bringer of death and enemy of truth, was grieved and rejoiced not. With his three daughters, Tanha, Raga and Arati, the tempters, and with his host of evil demons, he went to the place where the great samana sat. But Sakyamuni heeded him not. Mara uttered fear-inspiring threats and raised a whirlwind so that the skies were darkened and the ocean roared and trembled.

But the Blessed One under the Bodhi-tree remained calm and feared not. The Enlightened One knew that no harm could befall him.

The three daughters of Mara tempted the Bodhisattva, but he paid no attention to them, and when Mara saw that he could kindle no desire in the heart of the victorious samana, he ordered all the evil spirits at his command to attack him and overawe the great muni. But the Blessed One watched them as one would watch the harmless games of children. All the fierce hatred of the evil spirits was of no avail. The flames of hell became wholesome breezes of perfume, and the angry thunderbolts were changed into lotus-blossoms.

When Mara saw this, he fled away with his army from the Bodhi-tree, whilst from above a rain of heavenly flowers fell, and voices of good spirits were heard: "Behold the great muni! his heart unmoved by hatred. The wicked Mara's host 'gainst him did not prevail. Pure is he and wise, loving and full of mercy. As the rays of the sun drown the darkness of the world, so he who perseveres in his search will find the truth and the truth will enlighten him."

Enlightenment

THE Bodhisattva, having put Mara to flight, gave himself up to meditation. All the miseries of the world, the evils produced by evil deeds and the sufferings arising therefrom, passed before his mental eye, and he thought:

"Surely if living creatures saw the results of all their evil deeds, they would turn away from them in disgust. But selfhood blinds them, and they cling to their obnoxious desires. They crave pleasure for themselves and they cause pain to others; when death destroys their individuality, they find no peace; their thirst for existence abides and their selfhood reappears in new births.

Thus they continue to move in the coil and can find no escape from the hell of their own making. And how empty are their pleasures, how vain are their endeavours! Hollow like the plantain-tree and without contents like the bubble. The world is full of evil and sorrow, because it is full of lust. Men go astray because they think that delusion is better than truth. Rather than truth they follow error, which is pleasant to look at in the beginning but in the end causes anxiety, tribulation, and misery."

And the Bodhisattva began to expound the Dharma. The Dharma is the truth. The Dharma is the sacred law. The Dharma is religion. The Dharma alone can deliver us from error, from wrong and from sorrow.

Pondering on the origin of birth and death, the Enlightened One recognised that ignorance was the root of all evil; and these are the links in the development of life, called the twelve nidanas: In the beginning there is existence blind and without knowledge; and in this sea of ignorance there are stirrings formative and organising. From stirrings, formative and organising, rises awareness or feelings. Feelings beget organisms that live as individual beings. These organisms develop the six fields, that is, the five senses and the mind. The six fields come in contact with things. Contact begets sensation. Sensation creates the thirst of individualised being. The thirst of being creates a cleaving to things. The cleaving produces the growth and continuation of selfhood. Selfhood continues in renewed birth. The renewed births of selfhood are the causes of sufferings, old age, sickness, and death. They produce lamentation, anxiety, and despair.

The cause of all sorrow lies at the very beginning; it is hidden in the ignorance from which life grows. Remove ignorance and you will destroy the wrong desires that rise from ignorance; destroy these desires and you will wipe out the wrong perception that rises from them. Destroy wrong perception and there is an end of errors in individualised beings. Destroy the errors in individualised beings and the illusions of the six fields will disappear. Destroy illusions and the contact with things will cease to beget misconception. Destroy misconception and you do away with thirst. Destroy thirst and you will be free of all morbid cleaving. Remove the cleaving and you destroy the selfishness of selfhood. If the selfishness of selfhood is destroyed you will be above birth, old age, disease, and death, and you will escape all suffering.

The Enlightened One saw the four noble truths which point out the path that leads to Nirvana or the extinction of self: The first noble truth is the existence of sorrow. The second noble truth is the cause of suffering. The third noble truth is the cessation of sorrow. The fourth noble truth is the eightfold path that leads to the cessation of sorrow.

This is the Dharma. This is the truth. This is religion. And the Enlightened One uttered this stanza:

> "Through many births I sought in vain
> The Builder of this House of Pain.
> Now, Builder, You are plain to see,
> And from this House at last I'm free;
> I burst the rafters, roof and wall,
> And dwell in the Peace beyond them all."

There is self and there is truth. Where self is, truth is not. Where truth is, self is not. Self is the fleeting error of samsara; it is individual separateness and that egotism which begets envy and hatred. Self is the yearning for pleasure and the lust after vanity. Truth is the correct comprehension of things; it is the permanent and everlasting, the real in all existence, the bliss of righteousness.

The existence of self is an illusion, and here is no wrong in this world, no vice, no evil, except what flows from the assertion of self. The attainment of truth is possible only when self is recognised as an illusion. Righteousness can be practiced only when we have freed our mind from passions of egotism. Perfect peace can dwell only where all vanity has disappeared.

Blessed is he who has understood the Dharma. Blessed is he who does no harm to his fellow-beings. Blessed is he who overcomes wrong and is free from passion. To the highest bliss has he attained who has conquered all selfishness and vanity. He has become the Buddha, the Perfect One.

The First Converts

THE Blessed One tarried in solitude seven times seven days, enjoying the bliss of emancipation. At that time Tapussa and Bhallika, two merchants, came travelling on the road near by, and when they saw the great samana, majestic and full of peace, they approached him respectfully and offered him rice cakes and honey.

This was the first food that the Enlightened One ate after he attained Buddhahood.

And the Buddha addressed them and pointed out to them the way of salvation. The two merchants, seeing the holiness of the conqueror of Mara, bowed down in reverence and said: "We take our refuge, Lord, in the Blessed One and in the Dharma." Tapussa and Bhallika were the first that became followers of the Buddha and they were lay disciples.

The Brahma's Request

THE Blessed One having attained Buddhahood while resting under the shepherd's Nigrodha tree on the banks of the river Neranjara, pronounced this solemn utterance:

> "How sure his pathway in this wood,
> Who follows truth's unchanging call!
> How blessed, to be kind and good,
> And practice self-restraint in all!
> How light, from passion to be free,
> And sensual joys to let go by!
> And yet his greatest bliss will be
> When he has quelled the pride of 'I'.

"I have recognised the deepest truth, which is sublime and peace-giving' but difficult to understand; for most men move in a sphere of worldly interests and find their delight in worldly desires. The worldling will not understand the doctrine, for to him there is happiness in selfhood only, and the bliss that lies in a complete surrender to truth is unintelligible to him. He will call resignation what to the enlightened mind is the purest joy. He will see annihilation where the perfected one finds immortality. He will regard as death what the conqueror of self knows to be life everlasting. The truth remains hidden from him who is in the bondage of hate and desire. Nirvana remains incomprehensible and mysterious to the vulgar whose minds are beclouded with worldly interests. Should I preach the doctrine and mankind not comprehend it, it would bring me only fatigue and trouble."

Mara, the Evil One, on hearing the words of the Blessed Buddha, approached and said: "Be greeted, thou Holy One. Thou hast attained the highest bliss and it is time for thee to enter into the final Nirvana."

Then Brahma Sahampati descended from the heavens and, having worshiped the Blessed One, said: "Alas! the world must perish, should the Holy One, the Tathagata, decide not to teach the Dharma. Be merciful to those that struggle; have compassion upon the sufferers; pity the creatures who are hopelessly entangled in the snares of sorrow. There are some beings that are almost free from the dust of worldliness. If they hear not the doctrine preached, they will be lost. But if they hear it, they will believe and be saved."

The Blessed One, full of compassion, looked with the eye of a Buddha upon all sentient creatures, and he saw among them beings whose minds were but scarcely covered by the dust of worldliness, who were of good disposition and easy to instruct. He saw some who were conscious of the dangers of lust and wrong doing. And the Blessed One said to Brahma Sahampati: "Wide open be the door of immortality to all who have ears to hear. May they receive the Dharma with faith."

Then the Blessed One turned to Mara, saying: "I shall not pass into the final Nirvana, O Evil One, until there be not only brethren and sisters of an Order, but also lay disciples of both sexes, who shall have become true hearers, wise, well trained, ready and learned, versed in the scriptures, fulfilling all the greater and lesser duties, correct in life, walking according to the precepts- until they, having thus themselves learned the doctrine, shall be able to give information to others concerning it, preach it, make it known, establish it, open it, minutely explain it, and make it clear- until they, when others start vain doctrines, shall be able to vanquish and refute them, and so to spread the wonderworking truth abroad. I shall not die until the pure religion of truth shall have become successful, prosperous, widespread, and popular in all its full extent-until, in a word, it shall have been well proclaimed among men!"

Then Brahma Sahampati understood that the Blessed One had granted his request and would preach the doctrine

Upaka Sees The Buddha

NOW the Blessed One thought: "To whom shall I preach the doctrine first? My old teachers are dead. They would have received the good news with joy. But my five disciples are still alive. I shall go to them, and to them shall I first proclaim the gospel of deliverance."

At that time the five bhikkhus dwelt in the Deer Park at Benares, and the Blessed One rose and journeyed to their abode, not thinking of their unkindness in having left him at a time when he was most in need of their sympathy and help, but mindful only of the services which they had ministered unto him, and pitying them for the austerities which they practiced in vain.

Upaka, a young Brahman and a Jain, a former acquaintance of Siddhattha, saw the Blessed One while he journeyed to Benares, and, amazed at the majesty and sublime joyfulness of his appearance, said to him: "Thy countenance, my friend, is serene; thine eyes are bright and indicate purity and blessedness."

The holy Buddha replied: "I have obtained deliverance by the extinction of self. My body is chastened, my mind is free from desire, and the deepest truth has taken abode in my heart. I have obtained Nirvana, and this is the reason that my countenance is serene and my eyes are bright. I now desire to found the kingdom of truth upon earth, to give light to those who are enshrouded in darkness and to open the gate of deathlessness."

Upaka replied: "Thou professest then, friend, to be Jina, the conqueror of the world, the absolute one and the holy one."

The Blessed One said: "Jinas are all those who have conquered self and the passions of self; those alone are victorious who control their minds and abstain from evil. Therefore, Upaka, I am the Jina."

Upaka shook his head. "Venerable Gotama," he said, "thy way lies yonder," and taking another road he went away.

The Sermon At Benares

ON seeing their old teacher approach, the five bhikkus agreed among themselves not to salute him, nor to address him as a master, but by his name only. "For," so they said, "he has broken his vow and has abandoned holiness. He is no bhikkhu, but Gotama, and Gotama has become a man who lives in abundance and indulges in the pleasures of worldliness." But when the Blessed One approached in a dignified manner, they involuntarily rose from their seats and greeted him in spite of their resolution. Still they called him by his name and addressed him as "friend Gotama."

When they had thus received the Blessed One, he said: "Do not call the Tathagata by his name nor address him as 'friend,' for he is the Buddha, the Holy One. The Buddha looks with a kind heart equally on all living beings, and they therefore call him 'Father.' To disrespect a father is wrong; to despise him, is wicked. The Tathagata, the Buddha continued, does not seek salvation in austerities, but neither does he for that reason indulge in worldly pleasures, nor live in abundance. The Tathagata has found the middle path.

"There are two extremes, O bhikkhus, which the man who has given up the world ought not to follow-the habitual practice, on the one hand, of self-indulgence which is unworthy, vain and fit only for the worldly-minded and the habitual practice, on the other hand, of self-mortification, which is painful, useless and unprofitable."

"Neither abstinence from fish and flesh, nor going naked, nor shaving the head, nor wearing matted hair, nor dressing in a rough garment, nor covering oneself with dirt, nor sacrificing to Agni, will cleanse a man who is not free from delusions. Reading the Vedas, making offerings to priests, or sacrifices to the gods, self-mortification by heat or cold and many such penances performed for the sake of immortality, these do not cleanse the man who is not free from delusions. Anger, drunkenness, obstinacy, bigotry, deception, envy, self-praise, disparaging others, superciliousness and evil intentions constitute uncleanness; not verily the eating of flesh."

"A middle path, O bhikkhus avoiding the two extremes, has been discovered by the Tathagata-a path which opens the eyes, and bestows understanding, which leads to peace of mind, to the higher wisdom, to full enlightenment, to Nirvana! What is that middle path, O bhikkhus, avoiding these two extremes, discovered by the Tathagata-that path which opens the eyes, and bestows understanding, which leads to peace of mind, to the higher wisdom, to full enlightenment, to Nirvana? Let me teach you, O bhikkhus, the middle path, which keeps aloof from both extremes. By suffering, the emaciated devotee produces confusion and sickly thoughts in his mind. Mortification is not conducive even to worldly knowledge; how much less to a triumph over the senses!"

"He who fills his lamp with water will not dispel the darkness, and he who tries to light a fire with rotten wood will fail. And how can any one be free from self by leading a wretched life, if he does not succeed in quenching the fires of lust, if he still hankers after either worldly or heavenly pleasures? But he in whom self has become extinct is free from lust; he will desire neither worldly nor heavenly pleasures, and the satisfaction of his natural wants will not defile him. However, let him be moderate, let him eat and drink according to the need of the body."

"Sensuality is enervating; the self-indulgent man is a slave to his passions, and pleasure-seeking is degrading and vulgar. But to satisfy the necessities of life is not evil. To keep the body in good health is a duty, for otherwise we shall not be able to trim the lamp of wisdom, and keep our minds strong and clear. Water surrounds the lotus flower, but does not wet its petals. This is the middle path, O bhikkhus, that keeps aloof from both extremes." And the Blessed One spoke kindly to his disciples, pitying them for their errors, and pointing out the uselessness of their endeavours, and the ice of ill-will that chilled their hearts melted away under the gentle warmth of the Master's persuasion.

Now the Blessed One set the wheel of the most excellent law rolling, and he began to preach to the five bhikkhus, opening to them the gate of immortality, and showing them the bliss of Nirvana.

The Buddha said: "The spokes of the wheel are the rules of pure conduct: justice is the uniformity of their length; wisdom is the tire; modesty and thoughtfulness are the hub in which the immovable axle of truth is fixed. He who recognises the existence of suffering, its cause, its remedy, and its cessation has fathomed the four noble truths. He will walk in the right path."

"Right views will be the torch to light his way. Right aspirations will be his guide. Right speech will be his dwelling-place on the road. His gait will be straight, for it is right behaviour. His refreshments will be the right way of earning his livelihood. Right efforts will be his steps: right thoughts his breath; and right contemplation will give him the peace that follows in his footprints."

"Now, this, O bhikkhus, is the noble truth concerning suffering: Birth is attended with pain, decay is painful, disease is painful, death is painful. Union with the unpleasant is painful, painful is separation from the pleasant; and any craving that is unsatisfied, that too is painful. In brief, bodily conditions which spring from attachment are painful. This, then, O bhikkhus, is the noble truth concerning suffering."

"Now this, O bhikkhus, is the noble truth concerning the origin of suffering: Verily, it is that craving which causes the renewal of existence, accompanied by sensual delight, seeking satisfaction now here, now there, the craving for the gratification of the passions, the craving for a future life, and the craving for happiness in this life. This, then, O bhikkhus, is the noble truth concerning the origin of suffering."

"Now this, O bhikkhus, is the noble truth concerning the destruction of suffering: Verily, it is the destruction, in which no passion remains, of this very thirst; it is the laying aside of, the being free from, the dwelling no longer upon this thirst. This, then, O bhikkhus, is the noble truth concerning the destruction of suffering."

"Now, this, O bhikkhus, is the noble truth concerning the way which leads to the destruction of sorrow. Verily, it is this noble eightfold path; that is to say: Right views; right aspirations; right speech; right behaviour; right livelihood; right effort; right thoughts; and right contemplation. This, then, O bhikkhus, is the noble truth concerning the destruction of sorrow."

"By the practice of loving-kindness I have attained liberation of heart, and thus I am assured that I shall never return in renewed births. I have even now attained Nirvana."

When the Blessed One had thus set the royal chariot wheel of truth rolling onward, a rapture thrilled through all the universes. The devas left their heavenly abodes to listen to the sweetness of the truth; the saints that had parted from life crowded around the great teacher to receive the glad tidings; even the animals of the earth felt the bliss that rested upon the words of the Tathagata: and all the creatures of the host of sentient beings, gods, men, and beasts, hearing the message of deliverance, received and understood it in their own language.

And when the doctrine was propounded, the venerable Kondanna, the oldest one among the five bhikkhus, discerned the truth with his mental eye, and he said: "Truly, O Buddha, our Lord, thou hast found the truth!" Then the other bhikkhus too, joined him and exclaimed: "Truly, thou art the Buddha, thou hast found the truth."

And the devas and saints and all the good spirits of the departed generations that had listened to the sermon of the Tathagata, joyfully received the doctrine and shouted: "Truly, the Blessed One has founded the kingdom of righteousness. The Blessed One has moved the earth; he has set the wheel of Truth rolling, which by no one in the universe, be he god or man, can ever be turned back. The kingdom of Truth will be preached upon earth; it will spread; and righteousness, good-will, and peace will reign among mankind."

The Sangha Or Community

HAVING pointed out to the five bhikkhus the truth, the Buddha said: "A man that stands alone, having decided to obey the truth, may be weak and slip back into his old ways. Therefore, stand ye together, assist one another, and strengthen one another efforts. Be like unto brothers; one in love, one in holiness, and one in your zeal for the truth. Spread the truth and preach the doctrine in all quarters of the world, so that in the end all living creatures will be citizens of the kingdom of righteousness. This is the holy brotherhood; this is the church, the congregation of the saints of the Buddha; this is the Sangha that establishes a communion among all those who have taken their refuge in the Buddha."

Kondanna was the first disciple of the Buddha who had thoroughly grasped the doctrine of the Holy One, and the Tathagata looking into his heart said: "Truly, Kondanna has understood the truth." Therefore the venerable Kondanna received the name "Annata-Kondanna that is, "Kondanna who has understood the doctrine." Then the venerable Kondanna spoke to the Buddha and said: "Lord, let us receive the ordination from the blessed One." And the Buddha said: "Come, O bhikkhus! Well taught is the doctrine. Lead a holy life for the extinction of suffering."

Then Kondanna and the other bhikkhus uttered three times these solemn vows: "To the Buddha will I look in faith: He, the Perfect One, is holy and supreme. The Buddha conveys to us instruction, wisdom, and salvation; he is the Blessed One, who knows the law of being; he is the Lord of the world, who yoketh men like oxen, the Teacher of gods and men, the Exalted Buddha. Therefore, to the Buddha will I look in faith."

"To the doctrine will I look in faith: well-preached is the doctrine by the Exalted One. The doctrine has been revealed so as to become visible; the doctrine is above time and space. The doctrine is not based upon hearsay, it means 'Come and see'; the doctrine to welfare; the doctrine is recognised by the wise in their own hearts. Therefore to the doctrine will I look in faith."

"To the community will I look in faith; the community of the Buddha's disciples instructs us how to lead a life of righteousness;

the community of the Buddha's disciples teaches us how to exercise honesty and justice; the community of the Buddha's disciples shows us how to practice the truth. They form a brotherhood in kindness and charity, and their saints are worthy of reverence. The community of the Buddha's disciples is founded as a holy brotherhood in which men bind themselves together to teach the behests of rectitude and to do good. Therefore, to the community will I look in faith."

The gospel of the Blessed One increased from day to day, and many people came to hear him and to accept the ordination to lead thenceforth a holy life for the sake of the extinction of suffering. And the Blessed One seeing that it was impossible to attend to all who wanted to hear the truth and receive the ordination, sent out from the number of his disciples such as were to preach the Dharma, and said unto them:

"The Dharma and the Vinaya proclaimed by the Tathagata shine forth when they are displayed, and not when they are concealed. But let not this doctrine, so full of truth and so excellent, fall into the hands of those unworthy of it, where it would be despised and contemned, treated shamefully, ridiculed and censured. I now grant you, O bhikkhus, this permission. Confer henceforth in the different countries the ordination upon those who are eager to receive it, when you find them worthy."

"Go ye now, O bhikkhus, for the benefit of the many, for the welfare of mankind, out of compassion for the world. Preach the doctrine which is glorious in the beginning, glorious in the middle, and glorious in the end, in the spirit as well as in the letter. There are beings whose eyes are scarcely covered with dust, but if the doctrine is not preached to them they cannot attain salvation. Proclaim to them a life of holiness. They will understand the doctrine and accept it."

And it became an established custom that the bhikkhus went out preaching while the weather was good, but in the rainy season they came together again and joined their master, to listen to the exhortations of the Tathagata.

Yasa, The Youth Of Benares

AT that time there was in Benares a noble youth, Yasa by name, the son of a wealthy merchant. Troubled in his mind about the sorrows of the world, he secretly rose up in the night and stole away to the Blessed One. The Blessed One saw Yasa coming from afar. Yasa approached and exclaimed: "Alas, what distress! What tribulations!"

The Blessed One said to Yasa: "Here is no distress; here are no tribulations. Come to me and I will teach you the truth, and the truth will dispel your sorrows."

When Yasa, the noble youth, heard that there were neither distress, nor tribulations, nor sorrows, his heart was comforted. He went into the place where the Blessed One was, and sat down near him. Then the Blessed One preached about charity and morality. He explained the vanity of the thought "I am"; the dangers of desire, and the necessity of avoiding the evils of life in order to walk on the path of deliverance.

Instead of disgust with the world, Yasa felt the cooling stream of holy wisdom, and, having obtained the pure and spotless eye of truth, he looked at his person, richly adorned with pearls and precious stones, and his heart was shamed.

The Tathagata, knowing his inward thoughts, said: "Though a person be ornamented with jewels, the heart may have conquered the senses. The outward form does not constitute religion or affect the mind. Thus the body of a samana may wear an ascetic's garb while his mind is immersed in worldliness. A man that dwells in lonely woods and yet covets worldly vanities, is a worldling, while the man in worldly garments may let his heart soar high to heavenly thoughts. There is no distinction between the layman and the hermit, if but both have banished the thought of self."

Seeing that Yasa was ready to enter upon the path, the Blessed One said to him: "Follow me!" And Yasa joined the brotherhood, and having put on a bhikkhu's robe, received the ordination.

While the Blessed One and Yasa were discussing the doctrine, Yasa's father passed by in search of his son; and in passing he asked the Blessed One: "Pray, Lord, hast thou seen Yasa, my son?"

The Buddha said to Yasa's father: "Come in, sir, thou wilt find thy son"; and Yasa's father became full of joy and he entered. He sat down near his son, but his eyes were holden and he knew him not; and the Lord began to preach. And Yasa's father, understanding the doctrine of the Blessed One, said:

"Glorious is the truth, O Lord! The Buddha, the Holy One, our Master, sets up what has been overturned; he reveals what has been hidden; he points out the way to the wanderer who has gone astray; he lights a lamp in the darkness so that all who have eyes to see can discern the things that surround them. I take refuge in the Buddha, our Lord: I take refuge in the doctrine revealed by him: I take refuge in the brotherhood which he has founded. May the Blessed One receive me from this day forth while my life lasts as a lay disciple who has taken refuge in him." Yasa's father was the first lay-member who became the first lay disciple of the Buddha by pronouncing the three-fold formula of refuge.

When the wealthy merchant had taken refuge in the Buddha, his eyes were opened and he saw his son sitting at his side in a bhikkhu's robe. "My son, Yasa," he said, "thy mother is absorbed in lamentation and grief. Return home and restore thy mother to life."

Then Yasa looked at the Blessed One, who said: "Should Yasa return to the world and enjoy the pleasures of a worldly life as he did before?" Yasa's father replied: "If Yasa, my son, finds it a gain to stay with thee, let him stay. He has become delivered from the bondage of worldliness."

When the Blessed One had cheered their hearts with words of truth and righteousness, Yasa's father said: "May the Blessed One, O Lord, consent to take his meal with me together with Yasa as his attendant?" The Blessed One, having donned his robes, took his alms-bowl and went with Yasa to the house of the rich merchant. When they had arrived there, the mother and also the former wife of Yasa saluted the Blessed One and sat down near him.

Then the Blessed One preached, and the women having understood his doctrine, exclaimed: "Glorious is the truth, O Lord! We take refuge in the Buddha, our Lord. We take refuge in the doctrine revealed by him. We take refuge in the brotherhood which has been founded by him. May the Blessed One receive us from this day forth while our life lasts as lay disciples who have taken refuge in him." The mother and the wife of Yasa, the noble youth of Benares, were the first women who became lay disciples and took their refuge in the Buddha.

Now there were four friends of Yasa belonging to the wealthy families of Benares. Their names were Vimala, Subahu, Punnaji, and Gavampati.

When Yasa's friends heard that Yasa had cut off his hair and put on bhikkhu robes to give up the world and go forth into homelessness, they thought: "Surely that cannot be a common doctrine, that must be a noble renunciation of the world."

And they went to Yasa, and Yasa addressed the Blessed One saying: "May the Blessed One administer exhortation and instruction to these four friends of mine." And the Blessed One preached to them, and Yasa's friends accepted the doctrine and took refuge in the Buddha, the Dharma, and the Sangha.

Kassapa, The Fire-Worshipper

AT that time there lived in Uruvela the Jatilas, Brahman hermits with matted hair, worshipping the fire and keeping a fire-dragon; and Kassapa was their chief. Kassapa was renowned throughout all India, and his name was honoured as one of the wisest men on earth and an authority on religion. And the Blessed One went to Kassapa of Uruvela the Jatila, and said: "Let me stay a night in the room where you keep your sacred fire."

Kassapa, seeing the Blessed One in his majesty and beauty, thought to himself: "This is a great muni and a noble teacher. Should he stay overnight in the room where the sacred fire is kept, the serpent will bite him and he will die." And he said: "I do not object to your staying overnight in the room where the sacred fire is kept, but the serpent lives there; he will kill you and I should be sorry to see you perish."

But the Buddha insisted and Kassapa admitted him to the room where the sacred fire was kept. And the Blessed One sat down with body erect, surrounding himself with watchfulness. In the night the dragon came, belching forth in rage his fiery poison, and filling the air with burning vapour, but could do him no harm, and the fire consumed itself while the World-honoured One remained composed. And the venomous fiend became very wroth so that he died in his anger. When Kassapa saw the light shining forth from the room he said: "Alas, what misery! Truly, the countenance of Gotama the great Sakyamuni is beautiful, but the serpent will destroy him."

In the morning the Blessed One showed the dead body of the fiend to Kassapa, saying: "His fire has been conquered by my fire." And Kassapa thought to himself. "Sakyamuni is a great samana and possesses high powers, but he is not holy like me."

There was in those days a festival, and Kassapa thought: "The people will come hither from all parts of the country and will see the great Sakyamuni. When he speaks to them, they will believe in him and abandon me." And he grew envious. When the day of the festival arrived, the Blessed One retired and did not come to Kassapa. And Kassapa went to the Buddha on the next morning and said: "Why did the great Sakyamuni not come?"

The Tathagata replied: "Didst thou not think, O Kassapa, that it would be better if I stayed away from the festival?" And Kassapa was astonished and thought: "Great is Sakyamuni; he can read my most secret thoughts, but he is not holy like me."

The Blessed One addressed Kassapa and said: "Thou seest the truth, but acceptest it not because of the envy that dwells in thy heart. Is envy holiness? Envy is the last remnant of self that has remained in thy mind. Thou art not holy, Kassapa; thou hast not yet entered the path." And Kassapa gave up his resistance. His envy disappeared, and, bowing down before the Blessed One, he said: "Lord, our Master, let me receive the ordination from the Blessed One."

And the Blessed One said: "Thou, Kassapa, art chief of the Jatilas. Go, then, first and inform them of thine intention, and let them do as thou thinkest fit." Then Kassapa went to the Jatilas and said: "I am anxious to lead a religious life under the direction of the great Sakyamuni, who is the Enlightened One, the Buddha. Do as ye think best."

The Jatilas replied: "We have conceived a profound affection for the great Sakyamuni, and if thou wilt join his brotherhood, we will do likewise." The Jatilas of Uruvela now flung their paraphernalia of fire-worship into the river and went to the Blessed One.

Nadi Kassapa and Gaya Kassapa, brothers of the great Uruvela Kassapa, powerful men and chieftains among the people, were dwelling below on the stream, and when they saw the instruments used in fire-worship floating in the river, they said: "Something has happened to our brother. And they came with their folk to Uruvela. Hearing what had happened, they, too, went to the Buddha.

The Blessed One, seeing that the Jatilas of Nadi and Gaya, who had practiced severe austerities and worshiped fire, were now coming to him, preached a sermon on fire, and said: "Everything, O Jatilas, is burning. The eye is burning, all the senses are burning, thoughts are burning. They are burning with the fire of lust. There is anger, there is ignorance, there is hatred, and as long as the fire finds inflammable things upon which it can feed, so long will it burn, and there will be birth and death, decay, grief, lamentation, suffering, despair, and sorrow. Considering this, a disciple of the Dharma will see the four noble truths and walk in the eightfold path of holiness. He will become wary of his eye, wary of all his senses, wary of his thoughts. He will divest himself of passion and become free. He will be delivered from selfishness and attain the blessed state of Nirvana."

And the Jatilas rejoiced and took refuge in the Buddha, the Dharma, and the Sangha.

The Sermon At Rajagaha

THE Blessed One having dwelt some time in Uruvela went to Rajagaha, accompanied by a number of bhikkhus, many of whom had been Jatilas before. The great Kassapa, chief of the Jatilas and formerly a fire worshipper, went with him.

When the Magadha king, Seniya Bimbisara, heard of the arrival of Gotama Sakyamuni, of whom the people said, "He is the Holy One, the blessed Buddha, guiding men as a driver curbs bullocks, the teacher of high and low," he went out surrounded with his counsellors and generals and came to the grove where the Blessed One was. There they saw the Blessed One in the company of Kassapa, the great religious teacher of the Jatilas, and they were astonished and thought: "Has the great Sakyamuni placed himself under the spiritual direction of Kassapa, or has Kassapa become a disciple of Gotama?"

The Tathagata, reading the thoughts of the people, said to Kassapa: "What knowledge hast thou gained, O Kassapa, and what has induced thee to renounce the sacred fire and give up thine austere penances?"

Kassapa said: "The profit I derived from adoring the fire was continuance in the wheel of individuality with all its sorrows and vanities. This service I have cast away, and instead of continuing penances and sacrifices I have gone in quest of the highest Nirvana. Since I have seen the light of truth, I have abandoned worshipping the fire."

The Buddha, perceiving that the whole assembly was ready as a vessel to receive the doctrine, spoke thus to Bimbisara the king: "He who knows the nature of self and understands how the senses act, finds no room for selfishness, and thus he will attain peace unending. The world holds the thought of self, and from this arises false apprehension. Some say that the self endures after death, some say it perishes. Both are wrong and their error is most grievous. For if they say the self is perishable, the fruit they strive for will perish too, and at some time there will be no hereafter. Good and evil would be indifferent. This salvation from selfishness is without merit."

"When some, on the other hand, say the self will not perish, then in the midst of all life and death there is but one identity unborn and undying. If such is their self, then it is perfect and cannot be perfected by deeds. The lasting, imperishable self could never be changed. self would be lord and master, and there would be no use in perfecting the perfect; moral aims and salvation would be unnecessary."

"But now we see the marks of joy and sorrow. Where is any constancy? If there is no permanent self that does our deeds, then there is no self; there is no actor behind our actions, no perceiver behind our perception, no lord behind our deeds."

"Now attend and listen: The senses meet the object and from their contact sensation is born. Thence results recollection. Thus, as the sun's power through a burning-glass causes fire to appear, so through the cognisance born of sense and object, the mind originates and with it the ego, the thought of self, whom some Brahman teachers call the lord. The shoot springs from the seed; the seed is not the shoot; both are not one and the same, but successive phases in a continuous growth. Such is the birth of animated life."

"Ye that are slaves of the self and toil in its service from morn until night, ye that live in constant fear of birth, old age, sickness, and death, receive the good tidings that your cruel master exists not. Self is an error, an illusion, a dream. Open your eyes and awaken. See things as they are and ye will be comforted. He who is awake will no longer be afraid of nightmares. He who has recognised the nature of the rope that seemed to be a serpent will cease to tremble."

"He who has found there is no self will let go all the lusts and desires of egotism. The cleaving to things, covetousness, and sensuality inherited from former existences, are the causes of the misery and vanity in the world. Surrender the grasping disposition of selfishness, and you will attain to that calm state of mind which conveys perfect peace, goodness, and wisdom."

And the Buddha breathed forth this solemn utterance:

"Do not deceive, do not despise
Each other, anywhere.

Do not be angry, and do not
Secret resentment bear;
For as a mother risks her life
And watches over her child,
So boundless be your love to all,
So tender, kind and mild.
"Yea cherish good-will right and left,
For all, both soon and late,
And with no hindrance, with no stint,
From envy free and hate;
While standing, walking, sitting down,
Forever keep in mind:
The rule of life that's always best
Is to be loving-kind.

"Gifts are great, the founding of viharas is meritorious, meditations and religious exercises pacify the heart, comprehension of the truth leads to Nirvana, but greater than all is loving-kindness. As the light of the moon is sixteen times stronger than the light of all the stars, so loving-kindness is sixteen times more efficacious in liberating the heart than all other religious accomplishments taken together. This state of heart is the best in the world. Let a man remain steadfast in it while he is awake, whether he is standing, walking, sitting, or lying down."

When the Enlightened One had finished his sermon, the Magadha king said to the Blessed One: "In former days, Lord, when I was a prince, I cherished five wishes. I wished: O, that I might be inaugurated as a king. This was my first wish, and it has been fulfilled. Further, I wished: Might the Holy Buddha, the Perfect One, appear on earth while I rule and might he come to my kingdom. This was my second wish and it is fulfilled now. Further I wished: Might I pay my respects to him. This was my third wish and it is fulfilled now. The fourth wish was: Might the Blessed One preach the doctrine to me, and this is fulfilled now."

"The greatest wish, however, was the fifth wish: Might I understand the doctrine of the Blessed One. And this wish is fulfilled too."

"Glorious Lord! Most glorious is the truth preached by the Tathagata! Our Lord, the Buddha, sets up what has been overturned; he reveals what has been hidden; he points out the way to the wanderer who has gone astray; he lights a lamp in the darkness so that those who have eyes to see may see. I take my refuge in the Buddha. I take my refuge in the Dharma. I take my refuge in the Sangha."

The Tathagata, by the exercise of his virtue and by wisdom, showed his unlimited spiritual power. He subdued and harmonised all minds. He made them see and accept the truth, and throughout the kingdom the seeds of virtue were sown.

The King's Gift

SENIYA BIMBISARA, the king, having taken his refuge in the Buddha, invited the Tathagata to his palace, saying: "Will the Blessed One consent to take his meal with me tomorrow together with the fraternity of bhikkhus?" The next morning the king announced to the Blessed One that it was time for taking food: "Thou art my most welcome guest, O Lord of the world, come; the meal is prepared."

The Blessed One having donned his robes, took his alms-bowl and, together with a great number of bhikkhus, entered the city of Rajagaha. Sakka, the king of the Devas, assuming the appearance of a young Brahman, walked in front, and said: "He who teaches self-control with those who have learned self-control; the redeemer with those whom he has redeemed; the Blessed One with those to whom he has given peace, is entering Rajagaha. Hail to the Buddha, our Lord! Honour to his name and blessings to all who take refuge in him." Sakka intoned this stanza:

"Blessed is the place in which the Buddha walks,
And blessed the ears which hear his talks;
Blessed his disciples, for they are
The tellers of his truth both near and far.
"If all could hear this truth so good
Then all men's minds would eat rich food,
And strong would grow men's brotherhood."

When the Blessed One had finished his meal, and had cleansed his bowl and his hands, the king sat down near him and thought:

"Where may I find a place for the Blessed One to live in, not too far from the town and not too near, suitable for going and coming, easily accessible to all people who want to see him, a place that is by day not too crowded and by night not exposed to noise, wholesome and well fitted for a retired life? There is my pleasure-garden, the bamboo grove Veluvana, fulfilling all these conditions. I shall offer it to the brotherhood whose head is the Buddha."

The king dedicated his garden to the brotherhood, saying: "May the Blessed One accept my gift." Then the Blessed One, having silently shown his consent and having gladdened and edified the Magadha king by religious discourse, rose from his seat and went away.

Sariputta And Moggallana

AT that time Sariputta and Moggallana, two Brahmans and chiefs of the followers of Sanjaya, led a religious life. They had promised each other: "He who first attains Nirvana shall tell the other one."

Sariputta seeing the venerable Assaji begging for alms, modestly keeping his eyes to the ground and dignified in deportment, exclaimed: "Truly this samana has entered the right path; I will ask him in whose name he has retired from the world and what doctrine he professes." Being addressed by Sariputta, Assaji replied: "I am a follower of the Buddha, the Blessed One, but being a novice I can tell you the substance only of the doctrine."

Said Sariputta: "Tell me, venerable monk; it is the substance I want." And Assaji recited the stanza:

> "Nothing we seek to touch or see
> Can represent Eternity.
> They spoil and die: then let us find
> Eternal Truth within the mind."

Having heard this stanza, Sariputta obtained the pure and spotless eye of truth and said: "Now I see clearly, whatsoever is subject to origination is also subject to cessation. If this be the doctrine I have reached the state to enter Nirvana which heretofore has remained hidden from me." Sariputta went to Moggallana and told him, and both said: "We will go to the Blessed One, that he, the Blessed One, may be our teacher."

When the Buddha saw Sariputta and Moggallana coming from afar, he said to his disciples, "These two monks are highly auspicious." When the two friends had taken refuge in the Buddha, the Dharma and the Sangha, the Holy One said to his other disciples: "Sariputta, like the first-born O son of a world-ruling monarch, is well able to assist the king as his chief follower to set the wheel of the law rolling."

Now the people were annoyed. Seeing that many distinguished young men of the kingdom of Magadha led a religious life under the direction of the Blessed One, they became angry and murmured: "Gotama Sakyamuni induces fathers to leave their wives and causes families to become extinct." When they saw the bhikkhus, they reviled them, saying: "The great Sakyamuni has come to Rajagaha subduing the minds of men. Who will be the next to be led astray by him?"

The bhikkhus told it to the Blessed One, and the Blessed One said: "This murmuring, O bhikkhus, will not last long. it will last seven days. If they revile you, answer them with these words: 'It is by preaching the truth that Tathagatas lead men. Who will murmur at the wise? Who will blame the virtuous? Who will condemn self-control, righteousness, and kindness?" And the Blessed One proclaimed:

"Commit no wrong, do only good,
And let your heart be pure.
This is the doctrine Buddhas teach,
And this doctrine will endure."

Anathapindika, The Man Of Wealth

AT this time there was Anathapindika, a man of unmeasured wealth, visiting Rajagaha. Being of a charitable disposition, he was called "the supporter of orphans and the friend of the poor." Hearing that the Buddha had come into the world and was stopping in the bamboo grove near the city, he set out on that very night to meet the Blessed One.

And the Blessed One saw at once the sterling quality of Anathapindika's heart and greeted him with words of religious comfort. And they sat down together, and Anathapindika listened to the sweetness of the truth preached by the Blessed One. And the Buddha said: "The restless, busy nature of the world, this, I declare, is at the root of pain. Attain that composure of mind which is resting in the peace of immortality. Self is but a heap of composite qualities, and its world is empty like a fantasy."

"Who is it that shapes our lives? Is it Isvara, a personal creator? If Isvara be the maker, all living things should have silently to submit to their maker's power. They would be like vessels formed by the potter's hand; and if it were so, how would it be possible to practice virtue? If the world had been made by Isvara there should be no such thing as sorrow, or calamity, or evil; for both pure and impure deeds must come from him. If not, there would be another cause beside him, and he would not be self-existent. Thus, thou seest, the thought of Isvara is overthrown."

"Again, it is said that the Absolute has created us. But that which is absolute cannot be a cause. All things around us come from a cause as the plant comes from the seed; but how can the Absolute be the cause of all things alike? If it pervades them, then, certainly, it does not make them."

"Again, it is said that Self is the maker. But if self is the maker, why did it not make things pleasing? The causes of sorrow and joy are real and touchable. How can they have been made by self?"

"Again, if we adopt the argument that there is no maker, our fate is such as it is, and there is no causation, what use would there be in shaping our lives and adjusting means to an end? Therefore, we argue that all things that exist are not without cause. However, neither Isvara, nor the absolute, nor the self nor causeless chance, is the maker, but our deeds produce results both good and evil according to the law of causation."

"Let us, then, abandon the heresy of worshipping Isvara and of praying to him; let us no longer lose ourselves in vain speculations or profitless subtleties; let us surrender self and all selfishness, and as all things are fixed by causation, let us practice good so that good may result from our actions."

And Anathapindika said: "I see that thou art the Buddha, the Blessed One, the Tathagata, and I wish to open to thee my whole mind. Having listened to my words advise me what I shall do. My life is full of work, and having acquired great wealth, I am surrounded with cares. Yet I enjoy my work, and apply myself to it with all diligence. Many people are in my employ and depend upon the success of my enterprises."

"Now, I have heard thy disciples praise the bliss of the hermit and denounce the unrest of the world. 'The Holy One,' they say, 'has given up his kingdom and his inheritance, and has found the path of righteousness, thus setting an example to all the world how to attain Nirvana.' My heart yearns to do what is right and to be a blessing unto my fellows. Let me then ask thee, Must I give up my wealth, my home, and my business enterprises, and, like thyself, go into homelessness in order to attain the bliss of a religious life?"

And the Buddha replied: "The bliss of a religious life is attainable by every one who walks in the noble eightfold path. He that cleaves to wealth had better cast it away than allow his heart to be poisoned by it; but he who does not cleave to wealth, and possessing riches, uses them rightly, will be a blessing unto his fellows. It is not life and wealth and power that enslave men, but the cleaving to life and wealth and power. The bhikkhu who retires from the world in order to lead a life of leisure will have no gain, for a life of indolence is an abomination, and lack of energy is to be despised. The Dharma of the Tathagata does not require a man to go into homelessness or to resign the world, unless he feels called upon to do so; but the Dharma of the Tathagata requires every man to free himself from the illusion of self, to cleanse his heart, to give up his thirst for pleasure, and lead a life of righteousness. And whatever men do, whether they remain in the world as artisans, merchants, and officers of the king, or retire from the world and devote themselves to a life of religious meditation, let them put their whole heart into their task; let them be diligent and energetic, and, if they are like the lotus, which, although it grows in the water, yet remains untouched by the water, if they struggle in life without cherishing envy or hatred, if they live in the world not a life of self but a life of truth, then surely joy, peace, and bliss will dwell in their minds."

The Sermon On Charity

ANATHAPINDIKA rejoiced at the words of the Blessed One and said: "I dwell at Savatthi, the capital of Kosala, a land rich in produce and enjoying peace. Pasenadi is the king of the country, and his name is renowned among our own people and our neighbours. Now I wish to found there a vihara which shall be a place of religious devotion for your brotherhood, and I pray you kindly to accept it."

The Buddha saw into the heart of the supporter of orphans; and knowing that unselfish charity was the moving cause of his offer, in acceptance of the gift, the Blessed One said: "The charitable man is loved by all; his friendship is prized highly; in death his heart is at rest and full of joy, for he suffers not from repentance;

he receives the opening flower of his reward and the fruit that ripens from it. Hard it is to understand: By giving away our food, we get more strength, by bestowing clothing on others, we gain more beauty; by donating abodes of purity and truth, we acquire great treasures."

"There is a proper time and a proper mode in charity; just as the vigorous warrior goes to battle, so is the man who is able to give. He is like an able warrior a champion strong and wise in action. Loving and compassionate he gives with reverence and banishes all hatred, envy, and anger."

"The charitable man has found the path of salvation. He is like the man who plants a sapling, securing thereby the shade, the flowers, and the fruit in future years. Even so is the result of charity, even so is the joy of him who helps those that are in need of assistance; even so is the great Nirvana. We reach the immortal path only by continuous acts of kindliness and we perfect our souls by compassion and charity."

Anathapindika invited Sariputta to accompany him on his return to Kosala and help him in selecting a pleasant site for the vihara.

Jetavana, The Vihara

ANATHAPINDIKA, the friend of the destitute and the supporter of orphans, having returned home, saw the garden of the heir-apparent, Jeta, with its green groves and limpid rivulets, and thought: "This is the place which will be most suitable as a vihara for the brotherhood of the Blessed One." And he went to the prince and asked leave to buy the ground. The prince was not inclined to sell the garden, for he valued it highly. He at first refused but said at last, "If thou canst cover it with gold, then, and for no other price, shalt thou have it." Anathapindika rejoiced and began to spread his gold; but Jeta said: "Spare thyself the trouble, for I will not sell." But Anathapindika insisted. Thus they contended until they resorted to the magistrate.

Meanwhile the people began to talk of the unwonted proceeding, and the prince, hearing more of the details and knowing that Anathapindika was not only very wealthy but also straightforward and sincere, inquired into his plans. On hearing the name of the Buddha, the prince became anxious to share in the foundation and he accepted only one-half of the gold, saying: "Yours is the land, but mine are the trees. I will give the trees as my share of this offering to the Buddha."

Then Anathapindika took the land and Jeta the trees, and they placed them in trust of Sariputta for the Buddha. After the foundations were laid, they began to build the hall which rose loftily in due proportions according to the directions which the Buddha had suggested; and it was beautifully decorated with appropriate carvings. This vihara was called Jetavana, and the friend of the orphans invited the Lord to come to Savatthi and receive the donation. And the Blessed One left Kapilavatthu and came to Savatthi.

While the Blessed One was entering Jetavana, Anathapindika scattered flowers and burned incense, and as a sign of the gift he poured water from a golden dragon decanter, saying, "This Jetavana vihara I give for the use of the brotherhood throughout the world." The Blessed One received the gift and replied: "May all evil influences be overcome; may the offering promote the kingdom of righteousness and be a permanent blessing to mankind in general, to the land of Kosala, and especially also to the giver."

Then the king Pasenadi, hearing that the Lord had come, went in his royal equipage to the Jetavana vihara and saluted the Blessed One with clasped hands, saying: "'Blessed is my unworthy and obscure kingdom that it has met with so great a fortune. For how can calamities and dangers befall it in the presence of the Lord of the world, the Dharmaraja, the King of Truth. Now that I have seen thy sacred countenance, let me partake of the refreshing waters of thy teachings. Worldly profit is fleeting and perishable, but religious profit is eternal and inexhaustible. A worldly man, though a king, is full of trouble, but even a common man who is holy has peace of mind."

Knowing the tendency of the king's heart, weighed down by avarice and love of pleasure, the Buddha seized the opportunity and said: "Even those who, by their evil karma, have been born in low degree, when they see a virtuous man, feel reverence for him. How much more must an independent king, on account of merits acquired in previous existences, when meeting a Buddha, conceive reverence for him. And now as I briefly expound the law, let the Maharaja listen and weigh my words, and hold fast that which I deliver!"

"Our good or evil deeds follow us continually like shadows. That which is most needed is a loving heart! Regard thy people as men do an only son. Do not oppress them, do not destroy them;

keep in due check every member of thy body, forsake unrighteous doctrine and walk in the straight path. Exalt not thyself by trampling down others, but comfort and befriend the suffering. Neither ponder on kingly dignity, nor listen to the smooth words of flatterers."

"There is no profit in vexing oneself by austerities, but meditate on the Buddha and weigh his righteous law. We are encompassed on all sides by the rocks of birth, old age, disease, and death, and only by considering and practicing the true law can we escape from this sorrow-piled mountain. What profit, then, in practicing iniquity?"

"All who are wise spurn the pleasures of the body. They loathe lust and seek to promote their spiritual existence. When a tree is burning with fierce flames, how can the birds congregate therein? Truth cannot dwell where passion lives. He who does not know this, though he be a learned man and be praised by others as a sage, is beclouded with ignorance. To him who has this knowledge true wisdom dawns, and he will beware of hankering after pleasure. To acquire this state of mind, wisdom is the one thing needful. To neglect wisdom will lead to failure in life. The teachings of all religions should centre here, for without wisdom there is no reason."

"This truth is not for the hermit alone; it concerns every human being, priest and layman alike. There is no distinction between the monk who has taken the vows, and the man of the world living with his family. There are hermits who fall into perdition, and there are humble householders who mount to the rank of rishis. Hankering after pleasure is a danger common to all; it carries away the world. He who is involved in its eddies finds no escape. But wisdom is the handy boat, reflection is the rudder. The slogan of religion calls you to overcome the assaults of Mara, the enemy."

"Since it is impossible to escape the result of our deeds, let us practice good works. Let us guard our thoughts that we do no evil, for as we sow so shall we reap. There are ways from light into darkness and from darkness into light. There are ways, also, from the gloom into deeper darkness, and from the dawn into brighter light. The wise man will use the light he has to receive more light. He will constantly advance in the knowledge of truth."

"Exhibit true superiority by virtuous conduct and the exercise of reason; meditate deeply on the vanity of earthly things, and understand the fickleness of life. Elevate the mind, and seek sincere faith with firm purpose; transgress not the rules of kingly conduct, and let your happiness depend, not upon external things, but upon your own mind. Thus you will lay up a good name for distant ages and will secure the favour of the Tathagata."

The king listened with reverence and remembered all the words of the Buddha in his heart.

The Three Characteristics And The Uncreate

WHEN the Buddha was staying at the Veluvana, the bamboo grove at Rajagaha, he addressed the brethren thus: "Whether Buddhas arise, O priests, or whether Buddhas do not arise, it remains a fact and the fixed and necessary constitution of being that all conformations are transitory. This fact a Buddha discovers and masters, and when he has discovered and mastered it, he announces, publishes, proclaims, discloses, minutely explains and makes it clear that all conformations are transitory."

"Whether Buddhas arise, O priests, or whether Buddhas do not arise, it remains a fact and a fixed and necessary constitution of being, that all conformations are suffering. This fact a Buddha discovers and masters, and when he has discovered and mastered it, he announces, publishes, proclaims, discloses, minutely explains and makes it clear that all conformations are suffering.

"Whether Buddhas arise, O priests, or whether Buddhas do not arise, it remains a fact and a fixed and necessary constitution of being, that all conformations are lacking a self. This fact a Buddha discovers and masters, and when he has discovered and mastered it, he announces, teaches, publishes, proclaims, discloses, minutely explains and makes it clear that all conformations are lacking a self."

And on another occasion the Blessed One dwelt at Savatthi in the Jetavana, the garden of Anathapindika. At that time the Blessed One edified, aroused, quickened and gladdened the monks with a religious discourse on the subject of Nirvana. And these monks grasping the meaning, thinking it out, and accepting with their hearts the whole doctrine, listened attentively. But there was one brother who had some doubt left in his heart. He arose and clasping his hands made the request: "May I be permitted to ask a question?" When permission was granted he spoke as follows:

"The Buddha teaches that all conformations are transient, that all conformations are subject to sorrow, that all conformations are lacking a self. How then can there be Nirvana, a state of eternal bliss?"'

And the Blessed One, this connection, on that occasion, breathed forth this solemn utterance: "There is, O monks, a state where there is neither earth, nor water, nor heat, nor air; neither infinity of space nor infinity of consciousness, nor nothingness, nor perception nor non-perception; neither this world nor that world, neither sun nor moon. It is the uncreate. That O monks, I term neither coming nor going nor standing; neither death nor birth. It is without stability, without change; it is the eternal which never originates and never passes away. There is the end of sorrow."

"It is hard to realise the essential, the truth is not easily perceived; desire is mastered by him who knows, and to him who sees aright all things are naught. There is, O monks, an unborn, unoriginated, uncreated, unformed. Were there not, O monks, this unborn, unoriginated, uncreated, unformed, there would be no escape from the world of the born, originated, created, formed. Since, O monks, there is an unborn, unoriginated, uncreated and unformed, therefore is there an escape from the born, originated, created, formed."

The Regulations

LONG before the Blessed One had attained enlightenment, self-mortification had been the custom among those who earnestly sought for salvation. Deliverance of the soul from all the necessities of life and finally from the body itself, they regarded as the aim of religion. Thus, they avoided everything that might be a luxury in food, shelter, and clothing, and lived like the beasts in the woods. Some went naked, while others wore the rags cast away upon cemeteries or dung-heaps.

When the Blessed One retired from the world, he recognised at once the error of the naked ascetics, and, considering the indecency of their habit, clad himself in cast-off rags.

Having attained enlightenment and rejected all unnecessary self-mortifications, the Blessed One and his bhikkhus continued for a long time to wear the cast-off rags of cemeteries and dung-heaps. Then it happened that the bhikkhus were visited with diseases of all kinds, and the Blessed One permitted and explicitly ordered the use of medicines, and among them he even enjoined, whenever needed, the use of unguents. One of the brethren suffered from a sore on his foot, and the Blessed One enjoined the bhikkhus to wear foot-coverings.

Now it happened that a disease befell the body of the Blessed One himself, and Ananda went to Jivaka, physician to Bimbisara, the king. And Jivaka, a faithful believer in the Holy One, ministered unto the Blessed One with medicines and baths until the body of the Blessed One was completely restored.

At that time, Pajjota, king of Ujjeni, was suffering from jaundice, and Jivaka, the physician to king Bimbisara, was consulted. When King Pajjota had been restored to health, he sent to Jivaka a suit of the most excellent cloth. And Jivaka said to himself: "This suit is made of the best cloth, and nobody is worthy to receive it but the Blessed One, the perfect and holy Buddha, or the Magadha king, Senija Bimbisara."

Then Jivaka took that suit and went to the place where the Blessed One was; having approached him, and having respectfully saluted the Blessed One, he sat down near him and said: "Lord, I have a boon to ask of the Blessed One." The Buddha replied: "The Tathagatas, Jivaka, do not grant boons before they know what they are."

Jivaka said: "Lord, it is a proper and unobjectionable request."

"Speak, Jivaka," said the Blessed One.

"Lord of the world, the Blessed One wears only robes made of rags taken from a dung-heap or a cemetery, and so also does the brotherhood of bhikkhus. Now, Lord, this suit has been sent to me by King Pajjota, which is the best and most excellent, and the finest and the most precious, and the noblest that can be found. Lord of the world, may the Blessed One accept from me this suit, and may he allow the brotherhood of bhikkhus to wear lay robes."

The Blessed One accepted the suit, and after having delivered a religious discourse, he addressed the bhikkhus thus: "Henceforth ye shall be at liberty to wear either cast-off rags or lay robes. Whether ye are pleased with the one or with the other, I will approve of it."

When the people at Rajagaha heard, The Blessed One has allowed the bhikkhus to wear lay robes, those who were willing to bestow gifts became glad. And in one day many thousands of robes were presented at Rajagaha to the bhikkhus.

Suddhodana Attains Nirvana

WHEN Suddhodana had grown old, he fell sick and sent for his son to come and see him once more before he died; and the Blessed One came and stayed at the sick-bed, and Suddhodana, having attained perfect enlightenment, died in the arms of the Blessed One.

And it is said that the Blessed One, for the sake of preaching to his mother Maya-devi, ascended to heaven and dwelt with the devas. Having concluded his pious mission, he returned to the earth and went about again, converting those who listened to his teachings.

Women In The Sangha

YASODHARA had three times requested of the Buddha that she might be admitted to the Sangha, but her wish had not been granted. Now Pajapati, the foster-mother of the Blessed One, in the company of Yasodhara, and many other women, went to the Tathagata entreating him earnestly to let them take the vows and be ordained as disciples.

The Blessed One, foreseeing the danger that lurked in admitting women to the Sangha, protested that while the good religion ought surely to last a thousand years it would, when women joined it, likely decay after five hundred years; but observing the zeal of Pajapati and Yasodhara for leading a religious life he could no longer resist and assented to have them admitted as his disciples.

Then the venerable Ananda addressed the Blessed One thus: "Are women competent, venerable Lord, if they retire from household life to the homeless state, under the doctrine and discipline announced by the Tathagata, to attain to the fruit of conversion, to attain to a release from a wearisome repetition of rebirths, to attain to saintship?" The Blessed One declared: "Women are competent, Ananda, if they retire from household life to the homeless state, under the doctrine and discipline announced by the Tathagata, to attain to the fruit of conversion, to attain to a release from a wearisome repetition of rebirths, to attain to saintship."

"Consider, Ananda, how great a benefactress Pajapati has been. She is the sister of the mother of the Blessed One, and as foster-mother and nurse, reared the Blessed One after the death of his mother. So, Ananda, women may retire from household life to the homeless state, under the doctrine and discipline announced by the Tathagata."

Pajapati was the first woman to become a disciple of the Buddha and to receive the ordination as a bhikkhuni.

On Conduct Towards Women

THE bhikkhus came to the Blessed One and asked him: "O Tathagata, our Lord and Master, what conduct toward women dost thou prescribe to the samanas who have left the world?"

The Blessed One said: "Guard against looking on a woman. If ye see a woman, let it be as though ye saw her not, and have no conversation with her. If, after all, ye must speak with her, let it be with a pure heart, and think to yourself, 'I as a samana will live in this sinful world as the spotless leaf of the lotus, unsoiled by the mud in which it grows.'

"If the woman be old, regard her as your mother, if young, as your sister, if very young, as your child. The samana who looks on a woman as a woman, or touches her as a woman, has broken his vow and is no longer a disciple of the Tathagata. The power of lust is great with men, and is to be feared withal; take then the bow of earnest perseverance, and the sharp arrow-points of wisdom. Cover your heads with the helmet of right thought, and fight with fixed resolve against the five desires. Lust beclouds a man's heart, when it is confused with woman's beauty, and the mind is dazed."

"Better far with red-hot irons bore out both your eyes, than encourage in yourself sensual thoughts, or look upon a woman's form with lustful desires. Better fall into the fierce tiger's mouth, or under the sharp knife of the executioner, than dwell with a woman and excite in yourself lustful thoughts."

"A woman of the world is anxious to exhibit her form and shape, whether walking, standing, sitting, or sleeping. Even when represented as a picture, she desires to captivate with the charms of her beauty, and thus to rob men of their steadfast heart. How then ought ye to guard yourselves? By regarding her tears and her smiles as enemies, her stooping form, her hanging arms, and her disentangled hair as toils designed to entrap man's heart. Therefore, I say, restrain the heart, give it no unbridled license."

Visakha And Her Gifts

VISAKHA, a wealthy woman in Savatthi who had many children and grandchildren, had given to the order the Pubbarama or Eastern Garden, and was the first in Northern Kosala to become a matron of the lay sisters.

When the Blessed One stayed at Savatthi, Visakha went up to the place where the Blessed One was, and tendered him an invitation to take his meal at her house, which the Blessed One accepted. And a heavy rain fell during the night and the next morning; and the bhikkhus doffed their robes to keep them dry and let the rain fall upon their bodies.

When on the next day the Blessed One had finished his meal, she took her seat at his side and spoke thus: "Eight are the boons, Lord, which I beg of the Blessed One."

Said the Blessed One: "The Tathagatas, O Visakha, grant no boons until they know what they are." Visakha replied: "Befitting, Lord, and unobjectionable are the boons I ask."

Having received permission to make known her requests, Visakha said: "I desire, Lord, through all my life long to bestow robes for the rainy season on the Sangha, and food for incoming bhikkhus, and food for outgoing bhikkhus, and food for the sick, and food for those who wait upon the sick, and medicine for the sick and a constant supply of rice milk for the Sangha, and bathing robes for the bhikkhunis, the sisters." Said the Buddha: "But what circumstance is it, O Visakha, that thou hast in view in asking these eight boons of the Tathagata?"

Visakha replied: "I gave command, Lord, to my maidservant, saying, 'Go, and announce to the brotherhood that the meal is ready.' And the maid went, but when she came to the vihara, she observed that the bhikkhus had doffed their robes while it was raining, and she thought: 'These are not bhikkhus, but naked ascetics letting the rain fall on them. So she returned to me and reported accordingly, and I had to send her a second time. Impure, Lord, is nakedness, and revolting. It was this circumstance, Lord, that I had in view in desiring to provide the Sangha my life long with special garments for use in the rainy season."

"As to my second wish, Lord, an incoming bhikkhu, not being able to take the direct roads, and not knowing the place where food can be procured, comes on his way tired out by seeking for alms. It was this circumstance, Lord, that I had in view in desiring to provide the Sangha my life long with food for incoming bhikkhus. Thirdly, Lord, an outgoing bhikkhu, while seeking about for alms, may be left behind, or may arrive too late at the place whither he desires to go, and will set out on the road in weariness.

"Fourthly, Lord, if a sick bhikkhu does not obtain suitable food, his sickness may increase upon him, and he may die. Fifthly, Lord, a bhikkhu who is waiting upon the sick will lose his opportunity of going out to seek food for himself. Sixthly, Lord, if a sick bhikkhu does not obtain suitable medicines, his sickness may increase upon him, and he may die."

"Seventhly, Lord, I have heard that the Blessed One has praised rice-milk, because it gives readiness of mind, dispels hunger and thirst; it is wholesome for the healthy as nourishment, and for the sick as a medicine. Therefore I desire to provide the Sangha my life long with a constant supply of rice-milk."

"Finally, Lord, the bhikkhunis are in the habit of bathing in the river Achiravati with the courtesans, at the same landing-place, and naked. And the courtesans, Lord, ridicule the bhikkhunis, saying, 'What is the good, ladies, of your maintaining chastity when you are young? When you are old, maintain chastity then; thus will you obtain both worldly pleasure and religious consolation.' Impure, Lord, is nakedness for a woman, disgusting, and revolting. These are the circumstances, Lord, that I had in view."

The Blessed One said: "But what was the advantage you had in view for yourself, O Visakha, in asking the eight boons of the Tathagatha?"

Visakha replied: "Bhikkhus who have spent the rainy seasons in various places will come, Lord, to Savatthi to visit the Blessed One. And on coming to the Blessed One they will ask, saying: 'Such and such a bhikkhu, Lord, has died. What, now, is his destiny?' Then will the Blessed One explain that he has attained the fruits of conversion; that he has attained arahatship or has entered Nirvana, as the case may be."

"And I, going up to them, will ask, 'Was that brother, Sirs, one of those who had formerly been at Savatthi?' If reply to me, He has formerly been at Savatthi then shall I arrive at the conclusion, For a certainty did that brother enjoy either the robes for the rainy season, or the food for the incoming bhikkhus, or the food for the outgoing bhikkhus, or the food for the sick, or the food for those that wait upon the sick, or the medicine for the sick, or the constant supply of rice-milk."

"Then will gladness spring up within me; thus gladdened, joy will come to me; and so rejoicing all my mind will be at peace. Being thus at peace I shall experience a blissful feeling of content; and in that bliss my heart will be at rest. That will be to me an exercise of my moral sense, an exercise of my moral powers, an exercise of the seven kinds of wisdom! This Lord, was the advantage I had in view for myself in asking those eight boons of the Blessed One."

The Blessed One said: "It is well, it is well, Visakha. Thou hast done well in asking these eight boons of the Tathagata with such advantages in view. Charity bestowed upon those who are worthy of it is like good seed sown on a good soil that yields an abundance of fruits. But alms given to those who are yet under the tyrannical yoke of the passions are like seed deposited in a bad soil. The passions of the receiver of the alms choke, as it were, the growth of merits." And the Blessed One gave this thanks to Visakha:

"O noble woman of an upright life,
Disciple of the Blessed One, thou givest
Unstintedly in purity of heart.
Thou spreadest joy, assuagest pain,
And verily thy gift will be a blessing
As well to many others as to thee."

The Schism

WHILE the Blessed One dwelt at Kosambi, a certain bhikkhu was accused of having committed an offence, and, as he refused to acknowledge it, the brotherhood pronounced against him the sentence of expulsion.

Now, that bhikkhu was erudite. He knew the Dharma, had studied the rules of the order, and was wise, learned, intelligent, modest, conscientious, and ready to submit himself to discipline. And he went to his companions and friends among the bhikkhus, saying: "This is no offence, friends; this is no reason for a sentence of expulsion. I am not guilty. The verdict improper and invalid. Therefore I consider myself still as a member of the order. May the venerable brethren assist me in maintaining my right."

Those who sided with the expelled brother went to the bhikkhus who had pronounced the sentence, saying: "This is no offence"; while the bhikkhus who had pronounced the sentence replied: "This is an offense." Thus altercations and quarrels arose, and the Sangha was divided into two parties, reviling and slandering each other.

All these happenings were reported to the Blessed One. Then the Blessed One went to the place where the bhikkhus were who had pronounced the sentence of expulsion, and said to them: "Do not think, O bhikkhus, that you are to pronounce expulsion against a bhikkhu, whatever be the facts of the case, simply by saying: 'It occurs to us that it is so, and therefore we are pleased to proceed thus against our brother.' Let those bhikkhus who frivolously pronounce a sentence against a brother who knows the Dharma and the rules of the order, who is learned, wise, intelligent, modest, conscientious, and ready to submit himself to discipline, stand in awe of causing divisions. They must not pronounce a sentence of expulsion against a brother merely because he refuses to see his offense."

Then the Blessed One rose and went to the brethren who sided with the expelled brother and said to them: "Do not think, O bhikkhus, that if you have given offense you need not atone for it, thinking: 'We are without offense.' When a bhikkhu has committed an offense, which he considers no offense while the brotherhood consider him guilty, he should think: 'These brethren know the Dharma and the rules of the order; they are learned, wise, intelligent, modest, conscientious, and ready to submit themselves to discipline; it is impossible that they should on my account act with selfishness or in malice or in delusion or in fear.' Let him stand in awe of causing divisions, and rather acknowledge his offense on the authority of his brethren."

Both parties continued to keep Uposatha and perform official acts independently of one another; and when their doings were related to the Blessed One, he ruled that the keeping of Uposatha and the performance of official acts were lawful, unobjectionable, and valid for both parties. For he said: "The bhikkhus who side with the expelled brother form a different communion from those who pronounced the sentence. There are venerable brethren in both parties. As they do not agree, let them keep Uposatha and perform official acts separately."

And the Blessed One reprimanded the quarrelsome bhikkhus, saying to them: "Loud is the voice which worldings make; but how can they be blamed when divisions arise also in the Sangha? Hatred is not appeased in those who think: 'He has reviled me, he has wronged me, he has injured me.' For not by hatred is hatred appeased. Hatred is appeased by not-hatred. This is an eternal law.

"There are some who do not know the need of self-restraint; if they are quarrelsome we may excuse their behaviour. But those who know better, should learn to live in concord. If a man finds a wise friend who lives righteously and is constant in his character, he may live with him, overcoming all dangers, happy and mindful.

"But if he finds not a friend who lives righteously and is constant in his character, let him rather walk alone, like a king who leaves his empire and the cares of government behind him to lead a life of retirement like a lonely elephant in the forest. With fools there is no companionship. Rather than to live with men who are selfish, vain, quarrelsome, and obstinate let a man walk alone."

And the Blessed One thought to himself: "It is no easy task to instruct these headstrong and infatuate fools." And he rose from his seat and went away.

The Re-Establishment Of Concord

WHILST the dispute between the parties was not yet settled, the Blessed One left Kosambi, and wandering from place to place he came at last to Savatthi. In the absence of the Blessed One the quarrels grew worse, so that the lay devotees of Kosambi became annoyed and they said: "These quarrelsome monks are a great nuisance and will bring upon us misfortune. Worried by their altercations the Blessed One is gone, and has selected another abode for his residence. Let us, therefore, neither salute the bhikkhus nor support them. They are not worthy of wearing yellow robes, and must either propitiate the Blessed One, or return to the world."

And the bhikkhus of Kosambi, when no longer honoured and no longer supported by the lay devotees, began to repent and said: "Let us go to the Blessed One and let him settle the question of our disagreement." Both parties went to Savatthi to the Blessed One. And the venerable Sariputta, having heard of their arrival, addressed the Blessed One and said: "These contentious, disputatious, and quarrelsome bhikkhus of Kosambi, the authors of dissensions, have come to Savatthi. How am I to behave, O Lord, toward those bhikkhus."

"Do not reprove them, Sariputta," said the Blessed One, "For harsh words do not serve as a remedy and are pleasant to no one.

Assign separate dwelling-places to each party and treat them with impartial justice. Listen with patience to both parties. He alone who weighs both sides is called a muni. When both parties have presented their case, let the Sangha come to an agreement and declare the re-establishment of concord."

Pajapati, the matron, asked the Blessed One for advice, and the Blessed One said: "Let both parties enjoy the gifts of lay members, be they robes or food, as they may need, and let no one receive preference over any other."

The venerable Upali, having approached the Blessed One, asked concerning the re-establishment of peace in the Sangha: "Would it be right, O Lord," said he, "that the Sangha, to avoid further disputations, should declare the restoration of concord without inquiring into the matter of the quarrel?"

The Blessed One said: "If the Sangha declares the reestablishment of concord without having inquired into the matter, the declaration is neither right nor lawful. There are two ways of re-establishing concord; one is in the letter, and the other one is in the spirit and in the letter.

"If the Sangha declares the re-establishment of concord without having inquired into the matter, the peace is concluded in the letter only. But if the Sangha, having inquired into the matter and having gone to the bottom of it, decides to declare the re-establishment of concord, the peace is concluded in the spirit and also in the letter. The concord re-established in the spirit and in the letter is alone right and lawful."

And the Blessed One addressed the bhikkhus and told them the story of Prince Dighavu, the Long-lived. He said: "In former times, there lived at Benares a powerful king whose name was Brahmadatta of Kasi; and he went to war against Dighiti, the Long-suffering, a king of Kosala, for he thought, The kingdom of Kosala is small and Dighiti will not be able to resist my armies. And Dighiti, seeing that resistance was impossible against the great host of the king of Kasi, fled leaving his little kingdom in the hands of Brahmadatta; and having wandered from place to place, he came at last to Benares, and lived there with his consort in a potter's dwelling outside the town.

"The queen bore him a son and they called him Dighavu. When Dighavu had grown up, the king thought to himself: 'King Brahmadatta has done us great harm, and he is fearing our revenge; he will seek to kill us. Should he find us he will slay all three of us.' And he sent his son away, and Dighavu having received a good education from his father, applied himself diligently to learn all arts, becoming very skillful and wise.

"At that time the barber of King Dighiti dwelt at Benares, and he saw the king, his former master, and being of an avaricious nature, betrayed him to King Brahmadatta. When Brahmadatta, the king of Kasi, heard that the fugitive king of Kosala and his queen, unknown and in disguise, were living a quiet life in a potter's dwelling, he ordered them to be bound and executed; and the sheriff to whom the order was given seized King Dighiti and led him to the place of execution.

"While the captive king was being led through the streets of Benares he saw his son who had returned to visit his parents, and, careful not to betray the presence of his son, yet anxious to communicate to him his last advice, he cried: 'O Dighavu, my son! Be not far-sighted, be not near-sighted, for not by hatred is hatred appeased; hatred is appeased by not-hatred only.'

"The king and queen of Kosala were executed, but Dighavu their son bought strong wine and made the guards drunk. When the night arrived he laid the bodies of his parents upon a funeral pyre and burned them with all honours and religious rites. When King Brahmadatta heard of it, he became afraid, for he thought, Dighavu, the son of King Dighiti, is a wise youth and he will take revenge for the death of his parents. If he espies a favourable opportunity, he will assassinate me.'

"Young Dighavu went to the forest and wept to his heart's content. Then he wiped his tears and returned to Benares. Hearing that assistants were wanted in the royal elephants' stable, he offered his services and was engaged by the master of the elephants. And it happened that the king heard a sweet voice ringing through the night and singing to the lute a beautiful song that gladdened his heart. And having inquired among his attendants who the singer might be, was told that the master of the elephants had in his service a young man of great accomplishments, and beloved by all his comrades. They said, 'He is wont to sing to the lute, and he must have been the singer that gladdened the heart of the king.'

"The king summoned the young man before him and, being much pleased with Dighavu, gave him employment in the royal castle. Observing how wisely the youth acted, how modest he was and yet punctilious in the performance of his work, the king very soon gave him a position of trust. Now it came to pass that the king went hunting and became separated from his retinue, young Dighavu alone remaining with him. And the king worn out from the hunt laid his head in the lap of young Dighavu and slept.

"Dighavu thought: 'People will forgive great wrongs which they have suffered, but they will never be at ease about the wrong which they themselves have done. They will persecute their victims to the bitter end. This King Brahmadatta has done us great injury; he robbed us of our kingdom and slew my father and my mother. He is now in my power. Thinking thus he unsheathed his sword. Then Dighavu thought of the last words of his father. 'Be not far-sighted, be not near-sighted. For not by hatred is hatred appeased. Hatred is appeased by not-hatred alone.—Thinking thus, he put his sword back into the sheath.

"The king became restless in his sleep and he awoke, and when the youth asked, 'Why art thou frightened, O king?' he replied: 'My sleep is always restless because I often dream that young Dighavu is coming upon me with his sword. While I lay here with my head in thy lap I dreamed the dreadful dream again; and I awoke full of terror and alarm.' Then the youth, laying his left hand upon the defenceless king's head and with his right hand drawing his sword, said: 'I am Dighavu, the son of King Dighiti, whom thou hast robbed of his kingdom and slain together with his queen, my mother. I know that men overcome the hatred entertained for wrongs which they have suffered much more easily than for the wrongs which they have done, and so I cannot expect that thou wilt take pity on me; but now a chance for revenge has come to me.

"The king seeing that he was at the mercy of young Dighavu raised his hands and said: 'Grant me my life, my dear Dighavu, grant me my life. I shall be forever grateful to thee.' And Dighavu said without bitterness or ill-will: 'How can I grant thee thy life, O king, since my life is endangered by thee? I do not mean to take thy life. It is thou, O king, who must grant me my life."

"And the king said: 'Well, my dear Dighavu, then grant me my life, and I will grant thee thine.' Thus, King Brahmadatta of Kasi and young Dighavu granted each other's life and took each other's hand and swore an oath not to do any harm to each other.

"Then King Brahmadatta of Kasi said to young Dighavu: 'Why did thy father say to thee in the hour of his death: "Be not far-sighted, be not near-sighted, for hatred is not appeased by hatred.

Hatred is appeased by not-hatred alone,"-what did thy father mean by that?'

"The youth replied: 'When my father, O king, in the hour of his death said: 'Be not far-sighted," he meant, Let 'Be not hatred go far. And when my father said near-sighted," he meant, be not hasty to fall out with thy friends. And when he said For not by hatred is hatred appeased; hatred is appeased by not-hatred, he meant this: Thou hast killed my father and mother, O king, and if I should deprive thee of thy life, then thy partisans in turn would take away my life; my partisans again would deprive thine of their lives. Thus by hatred, hatred would not be appeased. But now, O king, thou hast granted me my life, and I have granted thee thine; thus by not-hatred hatred has been appeased.'

"Then King Brahmadatta of Kasi thought: 'How wise is young Dighavu that he understands in its full extent the meaning of what his father spoke concisely.' And the king gave him back his father's kingdom and gave him his daughter in marriage."

Having finished the story, the Blessed One said: "Brethren, ye are my lawful sons in the faith, begotten by the words of my mouth. Children ought not to trample under foot the counsel given them by their father; do ye henceforth follow my admonitions. Then the bhikkhus met in conference; they discussed their differences in mutual good will, and the concord of the Sangha was re-established.

The Bhikkhus Rebuked

IT happened that the Blessed One walked up and down in the open air unshod. When the elders saw that the Blessed One walked unshod, they put away their shoes and did likewise. But the novices did not heed the example of their elders and kept their feet covered.

Some of the brethren noticed the irreverent behaviour of the novices and told the Blessed One; and the Blessed One rebuked the novices and said: "If the brethren, even now, while I am yet living, show so little respect and courtesy to one another, what will they do when I have passed away?"

The Blessed One was filled with anxiety for the welfare of the truth; and he continued: "Even the laymen, O bhikkhus, who move in the world, pursuing some handicraft that they may procure them a living, will be respectful, affectionate, and hospitable to their teachers. Do ye, therefore, O bhikkhus, so let your light shine forth, that ye, having left the world and devoted your entire life to religion and to religious discipline, may observe the rules of decency, be respectful, affectionate, and hospitable to your teachers and superiors, or those who rank as your teachers and superiors. Your demeanour, O bhikkhus, does not conduce to the conversion of the unconverted and to the increase of the number of the faithful. It serves, O bhikkhus, to repel the unconverted and to estrange them. I exhort you to be more considerate in the future, more thoughtful and more respectful."

The Jealousy Of Devadatta

WHEN Devadatta, the son of Suprabuddha and a brother of Yasodhara, became a disciple, he cherished the hope of attaining the same distinctions and honours as Gotama Siddhattha. Being disappointed in his ambitions, he conceived in his heart a jealous hatred, and, attempting to excel the Perfect One in virtue, he found fault with his regulations and reproved them as too lenient.

Devadatta went to Rajagaha and gained the ear of Ajatasattu, the son of King Bimbisara. And Ajatasattu built a new vihara for Devadatta, and founded a sect whose disciples were pledged to severe rules and self-mortification.

Soon afterwards the Blessed One himself came to Rajagaha and stayed at the Veluvana vihara. Devadatta called on the Blessed One, requesting him to sanction his rules of greater stringency, by which a greater holiness might be procured. "The body," he said, "consists of its thirty-two parts and has no divine attributes. It is conceived in sin and born in corruption. Its attributes are liability to pain and dissolution, for it is impermanent. It is the receptacle of karma which is the curse of our former existences; it is the dwelling place of sin and diseases and its organs constantly discharge disgusting secretions. Its end is death and its goal the charnel house. Such being the condition of the body it behooves us to treat it as a carcass full of abomination and to clothe it in such rags only as have been gathered in cemeteries or upon dung-hills."

The Blessed One said: "Truly, the body is full of impurity and its end is the charnel house, for it is impermanent and destined to be dissolved into its elements. But being the receptacle of karma, it lies in our power to make it a vessel of truth and not of evil. It is not good to indulge in the pleasures of the body, but neither is it good to neglect our bodily needs and to heap filth upon impurities. The lamp that is not cleansed and not filled with oil will be extinguished, and a body that is unkempt, unwashed, and weakened by penance will not be a fit receptacle for the light of truth. Attend to your body and its needs as you would treat a wound which you care for without loving it. Severe rules will not lead the disciples on the middle path which I have taught. Certainly, no one can be prevented from keeping more stringent rules, if he sees fit to do so but they should not be imposed upon any one, for they are unnecessary."

Thus the Tathagata refused Devadatta's proposal; and Devadatta left the Buddha and went into the vihara speaking evil of the Lord's path of salvation as too lenient and altogether insufficient. When the Blessed One heard of Devadatta's intrigues, he said: "Among men there is no one who is not blamed. People blame him who sits silent and him who speaks, they also blame the man who preaches the middle path."

Devadatta instigated Ajatasattu to plot against his father Bimbisara, the king, so that the prince would no longer be subject to him. Bimbisara was imprisoned by his son in a tower, where he died, leaving the kingdom of Magadha to his son Ajatasattu.

The new king listened to the evil advice of Devadatta, and he gave orders to take the life of the Tathagata. However, the murderers sent out to kill the Lord could not perform their wicked deed, and became converted as soon as they saw him and listened to his preaching. The rock hurled down from a precipice upon the great Master split in twain, and the two pieces passed by on either side without doing any harm. Nalagiri, the wild elephant let loose to destroy the Lord, became gentle in his presence; and Ajatasattu, suffering greatly from the pangs of his conscience, went to the Blessed One and sought peace in his distress.

The Blessed One received Ajatasattu kindly and taught him the way of salvation; but Devadatta still tried to become the founder of a religious school of his own. Devadatta did not succeed in his plans and having been abandoned by many of his disciples, he fell sick, and then repented. He entreated those who had remained with him to carry his litter to the Buddha, saying: "Take me, children, take me to him; though I have done evil to him, I am his brother-in-law. For the sake of our relationship the Buddha will save me." And they obeyed, although reluctantly.

And Devadatta in his impatience to see the Blessed One rose from his litter while his carriers were washing their hands. But his feet burned under him; he sank to the ground; and, having chanted a hymn on the Buddha, died.

Name And Form

ON one occasion the Blessed One entered the assembly hall and the brethren hushed their conversation. When they had greeted him with clasped hands, they sat down and became composed. Then the Blessed One said: "Your minds are inflamed with intense interest; what was the topic of your discussion?"

And Sariputta rose and spake: "World-honoured master, were the nature of man's own existence. We were trying to grasp the mixture of our own being which is called Name and Form. Every human being consists of conformations, and there are three groups which are not corporeal. They are sensation, perception, and the dispositions; all three constitute consciousness and mind, being comprised under the term Name. And there are four elements, the earthy element, the watery element, the fiery element, and the gaseous element, and these four elements constitute man's bodily form, being held together so that this machine moves like a puppet. How does this name and form endure and how can it live?"

Said the Blessed One: "Life is instantaneous and living is dying. Just as a chariot-wheel in rolling rolls only at one point of the tire, and in resting rests only at one point; in exactly the same way, the life of a living being lasts only for the period of one thought. As soon as that thought has ceased the being is said to have ceased. As it has been said: 'The being of a past moment of thought has lived, but does not live, nor will it live. The being of a future moment of thought will live, but has not lived, nor does it live. The being of the present moment of thought does live, but has not lived, nor will it live.'

"As to Name and Form we must understand how they interact. Name has no power of its own, nor can it go on of its own impulse, either to eat, or to drink, or to utter sounds, or to make a movement. Form also is without power and cannot go on of its own impulse. It has no desire to eat, or to drink, or to utter sounds, or to make a movement. But Form goes on when supported by Name, and Name when supported by Form. When

Name has a desire to eat, or to drink, or to utter sounds, or to make a movement, then Form eats, drinks, utters sounds, makes a movement.

"It is as if two men, the one blind from birth and the other a cripple, were desirous of going travelling, and the man blind from birth were to say to the cripple as follows: 'See here! I am able to use my legs, but I have no eyes with which to see the rough and the smooth places in the road.' And the cripple were to say to the man blind from birth as follows: 'See here! I am able to use my eyes, but I have no legs with which to go forward and back.' And the man blind from birth, pleased and delighted, were to mount the cripple on his shoulders. And the cripple sitting on the shoulders of the man blind from birth were to direct him, saying, 'Leave the left and go to the right; leave the right and go to the left.'   "Here the man blind from birth is without power of his own, and weak, and cannot go of his own impulse or might. The cripple also is without power of his own, and weak, and cannot go of his own impulse or might. Yet when they mutually support one another it is not impossible for them to go. In exactly the same way Name is without power of its own, and cannot spring up of its own might, nor perform this or that action. Form also is without power of its own, and cannot spring up of its own might, nor perform this or that action. Yet when they mutually support one another it is not impossible for them to spring up and go on.

"There is no material that exists for the production of Name and Form; and when Name and Form cease, they do not go any whither in space. After Name and Form have ceased, they do not exist anywhere, any more than there is heaped-up music material. When a lute is played upon, there is no previous store of sound; and when the music ceases it does not go any whither in space. When it has ceased, it exists nowhere in a stored-up state. Having previously been non-existent, it came into existence on account of the structure and stern of the lute and the exertions of the performer; and as it came into existence so it passes away. In exactly the same way, all the elements of being, both corporeal and non-corporeal come into existence after having previously been non-existent; and having come into existence pass away.

"There is not a self residing in Name and Form, but the cooperation of the conformations produces what people call a man. Just as the word 'chariot' is but a mode of expression for axle, wheels, the chariot-body and other constituents in their proper combination, so a living being is the appearance of the groups with the four elements as they are joined in a unit. There is no self in the carriage and there is no self in man. O bhikkhus, this doctrine is sure and an eternal truth, that there is no self outside of its parts. This self of ours which constitutes Name and Form is a combination of the groups with the four elements, but there is no ego entity, no self in itself.

"Paradoxical though it may sound: There is a path to walk on, there is walking being done, but there is no traveller. There are deeds being done, but there is no doer. There is a blowing of the air, but there is no wind that does the blowing. The thought of self is an error and all existences are as hollow as the plantain tree and as empty as twirling water bubbles.

"Therefore, O bhikkhus, as there is no self, there is no transmigration of a self; but there are deeds and the continued effect of deeds. There is a rebirth of karma; there is reincarnation. This rebirth, this reincarnation, this reappearance of the conformations is continuous and depends on the law of cause and effect. Just as a seal is impressed upon the wax reproducing the configurations of its device, so the thoughts of men, their characters, their aspirations are impressed upon others in continuous transference and continue their karma, and good deeds will continue in blessings while bad deeds will continue in curses.

"There is no entity here that migrates, no self is transferred from one place to another; but there is a voice uttered here and the echo of it comes back. The teacher pronounces a stanza and the disciple who attentively listens to his teacher's instruction, repeats the stanza. Thus the stanza is reborn in the mind of the disciple. The body is a compound of perishable organs. It is subject to decay; and we should take care of it as of a wound or a sore; we should attend to its needs without being attached to it, or loving it. The body is like a machine, and there is no self in it that makes it walk or act, but the thoughts of it, as the windy elements, cause the machine to work. The body moves about like a cart. Therefore 'tis said:

"As ships are blown by wind on sails,
As arrows fly from twanging bow,
So, when the force of thought directs,
The body, following, must go.
Just as machines are worked by ropes,

So are the body's gear and groove;
Obedient to the pull of mind,
Our muscles and our members move.
No independent 'I' is here,
But many gathered mobile forces;
Our chariot is manned by mind,
And our karma is our horses.

"He only who utterly abandons all thought of the ego escapes the snares of the Evil One; he is out of the reach of Mara. Thus says the pleasure-promising tempter:

"So long as to those things
Called 'mine, and 'I' and 'me'
Your hungry heart still clings-
My snares you cannot flee.
"The faithful disciple replies:
"Naught's mine and naught of me,
The self I do not mind!
Thus Mara, I tell thee,
My path thou canst not find.

"Dismiss the error of the self and do not cling to possessions which are transient, but perform deeds that are good, for deeds are enduring and in deeds your karma continues.

"Since, then, O bhikkhus, there is no self, there can not be any after life of a self. Therefore abandon all thought of self. But since there are deeds and since deeds continue, be careful with your deeds. All beings have karma as their portion: they are heirs of their karma; they are sprung from their karma; their karma is their kinsman; their karma is their refuge; karma allots beings to meanness or to greatness.

"Assailed by death in life last throes
On quitting all thy joys and woes
What is thine own, thy recompense?
What stays with thee when passing hence?
What like a shadow follows thee
And will Beyond thine heirloom be?
Tis deeds, thy deeds, both good and bad;
Naught else can after death be had.
Thy deeds are thine, thy recompense;
They are thine own when going hence;
They like a shadow follow thee
And will Beyond thine heirloom be.

Let all then here perform good deeds,
For future weal a treasure store;
There to reap crops from noble seeds,
A bliss increasing evermore."

The Goal

THE Blessed One thus addressed the bhikkhus: "It is through not understanding the four noble truths, O bhikkhus, that we had to wander so long in the weary path of samsara, both you and I.

"Through contact thought is born from sensation, and is reborn by a reproduction of its form. Starting from the simplest forms, the mind rises and falls according to deeds, but the aspirations of a Bodhisattva pursue the straight path of wisdom and righteousness, until they reach perfect enlightenment in the Buddha.

"All creatures are what they are through the karma of their deeds done in former and in present existences.

"The rational nature of man is a spark of the true light; it is the first step on the upward road. But new births are required to insure an ascent to the summit of existence, the enlightenment of mind and heart, where the immeasurable light of moral comprehension is gained which is the source of all righteousness. Having attained this higher birth, I have found the truth and have taught you the noble path that leads to the city of peace. I have shown you the way to the lake of ambrosia, which washes away all evil desire. I have given you the refreshing drink called the perception of truth, and he who drinks of it becomes free from excitement, passion, and wrong-doing.

"The very gods envy the bliss of him who has escaped from the floods of passion and has climbed the shores of Nirvana. His heart is cleansed from all defilement and free from all illusion. He is like unto the lotus which grows in the water, yet not a drop of water adheres to its petals. The man who walks in the noble path lives in the world, and yet his heart is not defiled by worldly desires.

"He who does not see the four noble truths, he who does not understand the three characteristics and has not grounded himself in the uncreate, has still a long path to traverse by repeated births through the desert of ignorance with its mirages of illusion and through the morass of wrong. But now that you have gained comprehension, the cause of further migrations and aberrations is removed. The goal is reached. The craving of selfishness is destroyed, and the truth is attained. This is true deliverance; this is salvation; this is heaven and the bliss of a life immortal."

Miracles Forbidden

JOTIKKHA, the son of Subhadda, was a householder living in Rajagaha. Having received a precious bowl of sandalwood decorated with jewels, he erected a long pole before his house and put the bowl on its top with this legend: "Should a samana take this bowl down without using a ladder or a stick with a hook, or without climbing the pole, but by magic power, he shall receive as reward whatever he desires."

The people came to the Blessed One, full of wonder and their mouths overflowing with praise, saying: "Great is the Tathagata. His disciples perform miracles. Kassapa, the disciple of the Buddha, saw the bowl on Jotikkha's pole, and, stretching out his hand, he took it down, carrying it away in triumph to the vihara."

When the Blessed One heard what had happened, he went to Kassapa, and, breaking the bowl to pieces, forbade his disciples to perform miracles of any kind.

Soon after this it happened that in one of the rainy seasons many bhikkhus were staying in the Vajji territory during a famine. And one of the bhikkhus proposed to his brethren that they should praise one another to the householders of the village, saying: "This bhikkhu is a saint; he has seen celestial visions; and that bhikkhu possesses supernatural gifts; he can work miracles." And the villagers said: "It is lucky, very lucky for us, that such saints are spending the rainy season with us." And they gave willingly and abundantly, and the bhikkhus prospered and did not suffer from the famine.

When the Blessed One heard it, he told Ananda to call the bhikkhus together, and he asked them: "Tell me, O bhikkhus, when does a bhikkhu cease to be a bhikkhu?"

And Sariputta replied: "An ordained disciple must not commit any unchaste act. The disciple who commits an unchaste act is no longer a disciple of the Sakyamuni. Again, an ordained disciple must not take except what has been given him. disciple who takes, be it so little as a penny's worth, is no longer a disciple of the Sakyamuni. And lastly, an ordained disciple must not knowingly and malignantly deprive any harmless creature of life, not even an earthworm or an ant. The disciple who knowingly and malignantly deprives any harmless creature of its life is no longer a disciple of the Sakyamuni. These are the three great prohibitions."

And the Blessed One addressed the bhikkhus and said: "There is another great prohibition which I declare to you: An ordained disciple must not boast of any superhuman perfection. The disciple who with evil intent and from covetousness boasts of a superhuman perfection, be it celestial visions or miracles, is no longer a disciple of the Sakyamuni. I forbid you, O bhikkhus, to employ any spells or supplications, for they are useless, since the law of karma governs all things. He who attempts to perform miracles has not understood the doctrine of the Tathagata."

The Vanity Of Worldliness

THERE was a poet who had acquired the spotless eye of truth, and he believed in the Buddha, whose doctrine gave him peace of mind and comfort in the hour of affliction. It happened that an epidemic swept over the country in which he lived, so that many died, and the people were terrified. Some of them trembled with fright, and in anticipation of their fate were smitten with all the horrors of death before they died, while others began to be merry, shouting loudly, "Let us enjoy ourselves today, for we know not whether tomorrow we shall live"; yet was their laughter no genuine gladness, but a mere pretense and affectation.

Among all these worldly men and women trembling with anxiety, the Buddhist poet lived in the time of the pestilence, as usual, calm and undisturbed, helping wherever he could and ministering unto the sick, soothing their pains by medicine and religious consolation. And a man came to him and said:

"My heart is nervous and excited, for I see people die. I am not anxious about others, but I tremble because of myself. Help me; cure me of my fear."

The poet replied: "There is help for him who has compassion on others, but there is no help for thee so long as thou clingest to thine own self alone. Hard times try the souls of men and teach them righteousness and charity. Canst thou witness these sad sights around thee and still be filled with selfishness? Canst thou see thy brothers, sisters, and friends suffer, yet not forget the petty cravings and lust of thine own heart? Noticing the desolation in the

mind of the pleasure-seeking man, the Buddhist poet composed this song and taught it to the brethren in the vihara:

"Unless you take refuge in the Buddha and find rest in Nirvana,
Your life is but vanity-empty and desolate vanity.
To see the world is idle, and to enjoy life is empty.
The world, including man, is but like a phantom, and the hope of heaven is as a mirage.
"The worldling seeks pleasures, fattening himself like a caged fowl,
But the Buddhist saint flies up to the sun like the wild crane.
The fowl in the coop has food but will soon be boiled in the pot;
No provisions are given to the wild crane, but the heavens and the earth are his."

The poet said: "The times are hard and teach the people a lesson; yet do they not heed it." And he composed another poem on the vanity of worldliness:

"It is good to reform, and it is good to exhort people to reform.
The things of the world will all be swept away.
Let others be busy and buried with care.
My mind all unvexed shall be pure.
"After pleasures they hanker and find no satisfaction;
Riches they covet and can never have enough.
They are like unto puppets held up by a string.
When the string breaks they come down with a shock.
"In the domain of death there are neither great nor small;
Neither gold nor silver is used, nor precious jewels.
No distinction is made between the high and the low.
And daily the dead are buried beneath the fragrant sod.
"Look at the sun setting behind the western hills.
You lie down to rest, but soon the cock will announce morn.
Reform today and do not wait until it be too late
Do not say it is early, for the time quickly passes by.
"It is good to reform and it is good to exhort people to reform.
It is good to lead a righteous life and take refuge in the Buddha's name.
Your talents may reach to the skies, your wealth may be untold—
But all is in vain unless you attain the peace of Nirvana."

Secrecy And Publicity

THE Buddha said: "Three things, O disciples, are characterised by secrecy: love affairs, priestly wisdom, and all aberrations from the path of truth. Women who are in love, O disciples seek secrecy and shun publicity; priests who claim to be in possession of special revelation, O disciples, seek secrecy and shun publicity; all those who stray from the path of truth, O disciples, seek secrecy and shun publicity.

"Three things, O disciples, shine before the world and cannot be hidden. What are the three? The moon, O disciples, illumines the world and cannot be hidden; the sun, O disciples, illumines the world and cannot be hidden; and the truth proclaimed by the Tathagata illumines the world and cannot be hidden. These three things, O disciples, illumine the world and cannot be hidden. There is no secrecy about them."

The Annihilation Of Suffering

THE Buddha said: "What, my friends, is evil? Killing is evil; stealing is evil; yielding to sexual passion is evil; lying is evil; slandering is evil; abuse is evil; gossip is evil; envy is evil; hatred is evil; to cling to false doctrine is evil; all these things, my friends, are evil.

"And what, my friends, is the root of evil? Desire is the root of evil; hatred is the root of evil; illusion is the root of evil; these things are the root of evil.

"What, however, is good? Abstaining from killing is good; abstaining from theft is good; abstaining from sensuality is good; abstaining from falsehood is good; abstaining from slander is good; suppression of unkindness is good; abandoning gossip is good; letting go all envy is good; dismissing hatred is good; obedience to the truth is good; all these things are good.

"And what, my friend, is the root of the good? Freedom from desire is the root of the good; freedom from hatred and freedom from illusion; these things, my friends, are the root of the good.

"What, however, O brethren, is suffering? What is the origin of suffering? What is the annihilation of suffering? Birth is suffering; old age is suffering; disease is suffering; death is suffering; sorrow and misery are suffering; affliction and despair are suffering; to be united with loathsome things is suffering; the loss of that which we love and the failure in attaining that which is longed for are suffering; all these things, O brethren, are suffering.

"And what, O brethren, is the origin of suffering? It is lust, passion, and the thirst for existence that yearns for pleasure everywhere, leading to a continual rebirth I It is sensuality, desire, selfishness; all these things, O brethren, are the origin of suffering.

"And what is the annihilation of suffering? The radical and total annihilation of this thirst and the abandonment, the liberation, the deliverance from passion, that, O brethren, is the annihilation of suffering.

"And what, O brethren, is the path that leads to the annihilation of suffering? It is the holy eightfold path that leads to the annihilation of suffering, which consists of right views, right decision, right speech, right action, right living, right struggling, right thoughts, and right meditation.

"In so far, O friends, as a noble youth thus recognises suffering and the origin of suffering, as he recognises the annihilation of suffering, and walks on the path that leads to the annihilation of suffering, radically forsaking passion, subduing wrath, annihilating the vain conceit of the "I am, leaving ignorance, and attaining to enlightenment, he will make an end of all suffering even in this life."

Avoiding The Ten Evils

THE Buddha said: "All acts of living creatures become bad by ten things, and by avoiding the ten things they become good. There are three evils of the body, four evils of the tongue, and three evils of the mind.

"The evils of the body are, murder, theft, and adultery; of the tongue, lying, slander, abuse, and idle talk; of the mind, covetousness, hatred, and error.

"I exhort you to avoid the ten evils:
1. Kill not, but have regard for life.
2. Steal not, neither do ye rob; but help everybody to be master of the fruits of his labour.
3. Abstain from impurity, and lead a life of chastity.
4. Lie not, but be truthful. Speak the truth with discretion, fearlessly and in a loving heart.
5. Invent not evil reports, neither do ye repeat them. Carp not, but look for the good sides of your fellow-beings, so that ye may with sincerity defend them against their enemies.
6. Swear not, but speak decently and with dignity.

7. Waste not the time with gossip, but speak to the purpose or keep silence.
8. Covet not, nor envy, but rejoice at the fortunes of other people.
9. Cleanse your heart of malice and cherish no hatred, not even against your enemies; but embrace all living beings with kindness.
10. Free your mind of ignorance and be anxious to learn the truth, especially in the one thing that is needful, lest you fall a prey either to scepticism or to errors. Scepticism will make you indifferent and errors will lead you astray, so that you shall not find the noble path that leads to life eternal."

The Preacher's Mission

THE Blessed One said to his disciples: "When I have passed away and can no longer address you and edify your minds with religious discourse, select from among you men of good family and education to preach the truth in my stead. And let those men be invested with the robes of the Tathagata, let them enter into the abode of the Tathagata, and occupy the pulpit of the Tathagata.

"The robe of the Tathagata is sublime forbearance and patience. The abode of the Tathagata is charity and love of all beings. The pulpit of the Tathagata is the comprehension of the good law in its abstract meaning as well as in its particular application.

"The preacher must propound the truth with unshrinking mind. He must have the power of persuasion rooted in virtue and in strict fidelity to his vows. The preacher must keep in his proper sphere and be steady in his course. He must not flatter his vanity by seeking the company of the great, nor must he keep company with persons who are frivolous and immoral. When in temptation, he should constantly think of the Buddha and he will conquer. All who come to hear the doctrine, the preacher must receive with benevolence, and his sermon must be without invidiousness. The preacher must not be prone to carp at others, or to blame other preachers; nor speak scandal, nor propagate bitter words. He must not mention by name other disciples to vituperate them and reproach their demeanour.

"Clad in a clean robe, dyed with good colour, with appropriate undergarments, he must ascend the pulpit with a mind free from blame and at peace with the whole world. He must not take delight in quarrelous disputations or engage in controversies so as to show the superiority of his talents, but be calm and composed. No hostile feelings shall reside in his heart, and he must never abandon the disposition of charity toward all beings. His sole aim must be that all beings become Buddhas. Let the preacher apply himself with zeal to his work, and the Tathagata will show to him the body of the holy law in its transcendent glory. He shall be honoured as one whom the Tathagata has blessed. The Tathagata blesses the preacher and also those who reverently listen to him and joyfully accept the doctrine.

"All those who receive the truth will find perfect enlightenment. And, verily, such is the power of the doctrine that even by the reading of a single stanza, or by reciting, copying, and keeping in mind a single sentence of the good law, persons may be converted to the truth and enter the path of righteousness which leads to deliverance from evil. Creatures that are swayed by impure passions, when they listen to the voice, will be purified. The ignorant who are infatuated with the follies of the world will, when pondering on the profundity of the doctrine, acquire wisdom. Those who act under the impulse of hatred will, when taking refuge in the Buddha, be filled with good-will and love.

"A preacher must be full of energy, and cheerful hope, never tiring and never despairing of final success. A preacher must be like a man in quest of water who digs a well in an arid tract of land. So long as he sees that the sand is dry and white, he knows that the water is still far off. But let him not be troubled or give up the task as hopeless. The work of removing the dry sand must be done so that he can dig down deeper into the ground. And often the deeper he has to dig, the cooler and purer and more refreshing will the water be. When after some time of digging he sees that the sand be comes moist, he accepts it as a token that the water is near. So long as the people do not listen to the words of truth, the preacher knows that he has to dig deeper into their hearts; but when they begin to heed his words he apprehends that they will soon attain enlightenment.

"Into your hands, O you men of good family and education who take the vow of preaching the words of the Tathagata, the Blessed One transfers, intrusts, and commends the good law of truth.

Receive the good law of truth, keep it, read and re-read it, fathom it, promulgate it, and preach it to all beings in all the quarters of the universe.

"The Tathagata is not avaricious, nor narrow-minded, and he is willing to impart the perfect Buddha-knowledge unto all who are ready and willing to receive it. Do you be like him. Imitate him and follow his example in bounteously giving, showing, and bestowing the truth. Gather round you hearers who love to listen to the benign and comforting words of the law; rouse the unbelievers to accept the truth and fill them with delight and joy. Quicken them, edify them, and lift them higher and higher until they see the truth face to face in all its splendour and infinite glory."

When the Blessed One had thus spoken, the disciples said: "O thou who rejoicest in kindness having its source in compassion, thou great cloud of good qualities and of benevolent mind, thou quenchest the fire that vexeth living beings, thou pourest out nectar, the rain of the law! We shall do, O Lord, what the Tathagata commands. We shall fulfil his behest; the Lord shall find us obedient to his words."

And this vow of the disciples resounded through the universe, and like an echo it came back from all the Bodhisattvas who are to be and will come to preach the good law of Truth to future generations.

And the Blessed One said: "The Tathagata is like unto a powerful king who rules his kingdom with righteousness, but being attacked by envious enemies goes out to wage war against his foes. When the king sees his soldiers fight he is delighted with their gallantry and will bestow upon them donations of all kinds. Ye are the soldiers of the Tathagata, while Mara, the Evil One, is the enemy who must be conquered. And the Tathagata will give to his soldiers the city of Nirvana, the great capital of the good law. And when the enemy is overcome, the Dharma-raja, the great king of truth, will bestow upon all his disciples the most precious crown, which jewel brings perfect enlightenment, supreme wisdom, and undisturbed peace."

The Teacher

THIS is the Dharmapada, the path of religion pursued by those who are followers of the Buddha: Creatures from mind their character derive; mind-marshaled are they, mind-made. Mind is the source either of bliss or of corruption. By oneself evil is done; by oneself one suffers; by oneself evil is left undone; by oneself one is purified. Purity and impurity belong to oneself, no one can purify another. You yourself must make an effort. The Tathagatas are only preachers. The thoughtful who enter the way are freed from the bondage of Mara. He who does not rouse himself when it is time to rise; who, though young and strong, is full of sloth; whose will and thoughts are weak; that lazy and idle man will never find the way to enlightenment.

If a man hold himself dear, let him watch himself carefully; the truth guards him who guards himself. If a man makes himself as he teaches others to be, then, being himself subdued, he may subdue others; one's own self is indeed difficult to subdue. If some men conquer in battle a thousand times a thousand men, and if another conquer himself, he is the greatest of conquerors. It is the habit of fools, be they laymen or members of the clergy, to think, this is done by me. May others be subject to me. In this or that transaction a prominent part should be played by me." Fools do not care for the duty to be performed or the aim to be reached, but think of themselves alone. Everything is but a pedestal of their vanity.

Bad deeds, and deeds hurtful to ourselves, are easy to do; what is beneficial and good, that is very difficult. If anything is to be done, let a man do it, let him attack it vigorously!

Before long, alas! this body will lie on the earth, despised, without understanding, like a useless log; yet our thoughts will endure. They will be thought again, and will produce action. Good thoughts will produce good actions, and bad thoughts will produce bad actions.

Earnestness is the path of immortality, thoughtlessness the path of death. Those who are in earnest do not die; those who are thoughtless are as if dead already. Those who imagine they find truth in untruth, and see untruth in truth, will never arrive at truth, but follow vain desires. They who know truth in truth, and untruth in untruth, arrive at truth, and follow true desires. As rain breaks through an ill-thatched house, passion will break through an unreflecting mind. As rain does not break through a well-thatched house, passion will not break through a well-reflecting mind. lead the water wherever they like; fletchers bend the arrow; carpenters bend a log of wood; wise people fashion themselves; wise people falter not amidst blame and praise. Having listened to the law, they become serene, like a deep, smooth, and still lake.

If a man speaks or acts with an evil thought, pain follows him as the wheel follows the foot of the ox that draws the wagon. An evil deed is better left undone, for a man will repent of it afterwards; a good deed is better done, for having done it one will not repent. If a man commits a wrong let him not do it again; let him not delight in wrongdoing; pain is the outcome of evil. If a man does what is good, let him do it again; let him delight in it; happiness is the outcome of good.

Let no man think lightly of evil, saying in his heart, It will not come nigh unto me."As by the falling of waterdrops a water-pot is filled, so the fool becomes full of evil, though he gather it little by little. Let no man think lightly of good, saying in his heart, It will not come nigh unto me." As by the falling of water-drops a water-pot is filled, so the wise man becomes full of good, though he gather it little by little.

He who lives for pleasure only, his senses uncontrolled, immoderate in his food, idle, and weak, him Mara, the tempter, will certainly overthrow, as the wind throws down a weak tree. He who lives without looking for pleasures, his senses well-controlled, moderate in his food, faithful and strong, him Mara will certainly not overthrow, any more than the wind throws down a rocky mountain.

The fool who knows his foolishness, is wise at least so far. But a fool who thinks himself wise, he is a fool indeed. To the evil-doer wrong appears sweet as honey; he looks upon it as pleasant so long as it bears no fruit; but when its fruit ripens, then he looks upon it as wrong. And so the good man looks upon the goodness of the Dharma as a burden and an evil so long as it bears no fruit; but when its fruit ripens, then he sees its goodness.

A hater may do great harm to a hater, or an enemy to an enemy; but a wrongly-directed mind will do greater mischief unto itself. A mother, a father, or any other relative will do much good; but a well-directed mind will do greater service unto itself.

He whose wickedness is very great brings himself down to that state where his enemy wishes him to be. He himself is his greatest enemy. Thus a creeper destroys the life of a tree on which it finds support.

Do not direct thy thought to what gives pleasure, that thou mayest not cry out when burning, "This is pain." The wicked man burns by his own deeds, as if burnt by fire. Pleasures destroy the foolish; the foolish man by his thirst for pleasures destroys himself as if he were his own enemy. The fields are damaged by hurricanes and weeds; mankind is damaged by passion, by hatred, by vanity, and by lust. Let no man ever take into consideration whether a thing is pleasant or unpleasant. The love of pleasure begets grief and the dread of pain causes fear; he who is free from the love of pleasure and the dread of pain knows neither grief nor fear.

He who gives himself to vanity, and does not give himself to meditation, forgetting the real aim of life and grasping at pleasure, will in time envy him who has exerted himself in meditation. The fault of others is easily noticed, but that of oneself is difficult to perceive. A man winnows his neighbour's faults like chaff, but his own fault he hides, as a cheat hides the false die from the gambler. If a man looks after the faults of others, and is always inclined to take offense, his own passions will grow, and he is far from the destruction of passions. Not about the perversities of others, not about their sins of commission or omission, but about his own misdeeds and negligences alone should a sage be worried. Good people shine from afar, like the snowy mountains; bad people are concealed, like arrows shot by night.

If a man by causing pain to others, wishes to obtain pleasure for himself, he, entangled in the bonds of selfishness, will never be free from hatred. Let a man overcome anger by love, let him overcome evil by good; let him overcome the greedy by liberality, the liar by truth! For hatred does not cease by hatred at any time; hatred ceases by not hatred, this is an old rule.

Speak the truth, do not yield to anger; give, if thou art asked; by these three steps thou wilt become divine. Let a wise man blow off the impurities of his self, as a smith blows off the impurities of silver, one by one, little by little, and from time to time.

Lead others, not by violence, but by righteousness and equity. He who possesses virtue and intelligence, who is just, speaks the truth, and does what is his own business, him the world will hold dear. As the bee collects nectar and departs without injuring the flower, or its colour or scent, so let a sage dwell in the community.

If a traveller does not meet with one who is his better, or his equal, let him firmly keep to his solitary journey; there is no companionship with fools. Long is the night to him who is awake; long is a mile to him who is tired; long is life to the foolish who do not know the true religion. Better than living a hundred years not seeing the highest truth, is one day in the life of a man who sees the highest truth.

Some form their Dharma arbitrarily and fabricate it artificially; they advance complex speculations and imagine that good results are attainable only by the acceptance of their theories; yet the truth is but one; there are not different truths in the world. Having reflected on the various theories, we have gone into the yoke with him who has shaken off all sin. But shall we be able to proceed together with him?

The best of ways is the eightfold path. This is the path. There is no other that leads to the purifying of intelligence. Go on this path! Everything else is the deceit of Mara, the tempter. If you go on this path, you will make an end of pain! Says the Tathagata, The path was preached by me, when I had understood the removal of the thorn in the flesh.

Not only by discipline and vows, not only by much learning, do I earn the happiness of release which no worldling can know. Bhikkhu, be not confident as long as thou hast not attained the extinction of thirst. The extinction of evil desire is the highest religion.

The gift of religion exceeds all gifts; the sweetness of religion exceeds all sweetness; the delight in religion exceeds all delights; the extinction of thirst overcomes all pain. Few are there among men who cross the river and reach the goal. The great multitudes are running up and down the shore; but there is no suffering for him who has finished his journey.

As the lily will grow full of sweet perfume and delight upon a heap of rubbish, thus the disciple of the truly enlightened Buddha shines forth by his wisdom among those who are like rubbish, among the people that walk in darkness. Let us live happily then, not hating those who hate us! Among men who hate us let us dwell free from hatred!

Let us live happily then, free from all ailments among the ailing! Among men who are ailing let us dwell free from ailments! Let us live happily, then, free from greed among the greedy! Among men who are greedy let us dwell free from greed!

The sun is bright by day, the moon shines by night, the warrior is bright in his armour thinkers are bright in their meditation; but among all, the brightest, with splendour day and night, is the Buddha, the Awakened, the Holy, Blessed.

The Two Brahmans

AT one time when the Blessed One was journeying through Kosala he came to the Brahman village which is called Manasakata. There he stayed in a mango grove. And two young Brahmans came to him who were of different schools. One was named Vasettha and the other Bharadvaja. And Vasettha said to the Blessed One:

"We have a dispute as to the true path. I say the straight path which leads unto a union with Brahma is that which has been announced by the Brahman Pokkharasati, while my friend says the straight path which leads unto a union with Brahma is that which has been announced by the Brahman Tarukkha. Now, regarding thy high reputation, O samana, and knowing that thou art called the Enlightened One, the teacher of men and gods, the Blessed Buddha, we have come to ask thee, are all these paths salvation? There are many roads all around our village, and all lead to Manasakata. Is it just so with the paths of the sages? Are all paths to salvation, and do they all lead to a union with Brahma?"

Then the Blessed One proposed these questions to the two Brahmans: "Do you think that all paths are right?" Both answered and said: "Yes, Gotama, we think so."

"But tell me," continued the Buddha "has any one of the Brahmans, versed in the Vedas, seen Brahma face to face?" "No sir!" was the reply.

"But, then," said the Blessed One, "has any teacher of the Brahmans, versed in the Vedas, seen Brahma face to face?" The two Brahmans said: "No, sir."

"But, then," said the Blessed One, has any one of the authors of the Vedas seen Brahma face to face?" Again the two Brahmans answered in the negative and exclaimed: "How can any one see Brahma or understand him, for the mortal cannot understand the immortal." And the Blessed One proposed an illustration, saying:

"It is as if a man should make a staircase in the place where four roads cross, to mount up into a mansion. And people should ask him, Where, good friends, is this mansion, to mount up into which you are making this staircase? Knowest thou whether it is in the east, or in the south, or in the west, or in the north? Whether it is high, or low, or of medium size?' And when so asked he should answer, 'I know it not.' And people should say to him, 'But, then, good friend, thou art making a staircase to mount up into something-taking it for a mansion-which all the while thou knowest not, neither hast thou seen it.' And when so asked he should answer, That is exactly what I do; yea I know that I cannot know it.' What would you think of him? Would you not say that the talk of that man was foolish talk?"

"In sooth, Gotama," said the two Brahmans, "it be foolish talk!" The Blessed One continued: "Then the Brahmans should say, 'We show you the way unto a union with what we know not and what we have not seen." This being the substance of Brahman lore, does it not follow that their task is vain?"

"It does follow," replied Bharadvaja.

Said the Blessed One: "Thus it is impossible that Brahmans versed in the three Vedas should be able to show the way to a state of union with that which they neither know nor have seen. Just as when a string of blind men are clinging one to the other. Neither can the foremost see, nor can those in the middle see, nor can the hindmost see. Even so, methinks the talk of the Brahmans versed in the three Vedas is but blind talk; it is ridiculous, consists of mere words, and is a vain and empty thing. "Now suppose," added the Blessed One "that a man should come hither to the bank of the river, and, having some business on the other side, should want to cross. Do you suppose that if he were to invoke the other bank of the river to come over to him on this side, the bank would come on account of his praying?"

"Certainly not, Gotama."

"Yet this is the way of the Brahmans. They omit the practice of those qualities which really make a man a Brahman, and say, 'Indra, we call upon thee; Soma, we call upon thee; Varuna, we call upon thee; Brahma, we call upon thee.' Verily, it is not possible that these Brahmans, on account of their invocations, prayers, and praises, should after death be united with Brahma.

"Now tell me," continued the Buddha, "what do the Brahmans say of Brahma? Is his mind full of lust?" And when the Brahmans denied this, the Buddha asked: "Is Brahma's mind full of malice, sloth, or pride?"

"No sir!" was the reply. "He is the opposite of all this."

And the Buddha went on: "But are the Brahmans free from these vices?" "No, sir!" said Vasettha.

The Holy One said: "The Brahmans cling to the five things leading to worldliness and yield to the temptations of the senses; they are entangled in the five hindrances, lust, malice, sloth, pride, and doubt. How can they be united to that which is most unlike their nature? Therefore the threefold wisdom of the Brahmans is a waterless desert, a pathless jungle, and a hopeless desolation."

When the Buddha had thus spoken, one of the Brahmans said: "We are told, Gotama, that the Sakyamuni knows the path to a union with Brahma."

And the Blessed One said: "What do you think, O Brahmans, of a man born and brought up in Manasakata? Would he be in doubt about the most direct way from this spot to Manasakata?"

"Certainly not, Gotama."

"Thus," replied the Buddha, "the Tathagata knows the straight path that leads to a union with Brahma. He knows it as one who has entered the world of Brahma and has been born in it. There can be no doubt in the Tathagata."

The two young Brahmans said: "If thou knowest the way show it to us."

And the Buddha said: "The Tathagata sees the universe face to face and understands its nature. He proclaims the truth both in its letter and in its spirit, and his doctrine is glorious in its origin, glorious in its progress, glorious in its consummation. The Tathagata reveals the higher life in its purity and perfection. He can show you the way to that which is contrary to the five great hindrances. The Tathagata lets his mind pervade the four quarters of the world with thoughts of love. And thus the whole wide world, above, below, around, and everywhere will continue to be filled with love, far-reaching, grown great, and beyond measure. just as a mighty trumpeter makes himself heard-and that without difficulty-in all the four quarters of the earth; even so is the coming of the Tathagata: there is not one living creature that the Tathagata passes by or leaves aside, but regards them all with mind set free, and deep-felt love.

"This is the sign that a man follows the right path: Uprightness is his delight, and he sees danger in the least of those things which he should avoid. He trains himself in the commands of morality, he encompasseth himself with holiness in word and deed; he sustains his life by means that are quite pure; good is his conduct, guarded is the door of his senses; mindful and self-possessed, he is altogether happy. He who walks in the eightfold noble path with unswerving determination is sure to reach Nirvana. The Tathagata anxiously watches over his children and with loving care helps them to see the light.

"When a hen has eight or ten or twelve eggs, over which she has properly brooded, the wish arises in her heart, 'O would that my little chickens would break open the eggshell with their claws, or with their beaks, and come forth into the light in safety!' yet all the while those little chickens are sure to break the egg-shell and will come forth into the light in safety. Even so, a brother who with firm determination walks in the noble path is sure to come forth into the light, sure to reach up to the higher wisdom, sure to attain to the highest bliss of enlightenment."

Guard The Six Quarters

WHILE the Blessed One was staying at the bamboo grove near Rajagaha, he once met on his way Sigala, a householder, who, clasping his hands, turned to the four quarters of the world, to the zenith above, and to the nadir below. The Blessed One, knowing that this was done according to the traditional religious superstition to avert evil, asked Sigala: "Why performest thou these strange ceremonies?"

And Sigala in reply said: "Dost thou think it strange that I protect my home against the influences of demons? I know thou wouldst fain tell me, O Gotama Sakyamuni, whom people call the Tathagata and the Blessed Buddha, that incantations are of no avail and possess no saving power. But listen to me and know, that in performing this rite I honour, reverence, and keep sacred the words of my father."

Then the Tathagata said: "Thou dost well, O Sigala, to honour, reverence, and keep sacred the words of thy father; and it is thy duty to protect thy home, thy wife, thy children, and thy children's children against the hurtful influences of evil spirits. I find no fault with the performance of thy father's rite. But I find that thou dost not understand the ceremony. Let the Tathagata, who now speaks to thee as a spiritual father and loves thee no less than did thy parents, explain to thee the meaning of the six directions.

"To guard thy home by mysterious ceremonies is not sufficient; thou must guard it by good deeds. Turn to thy parents in the East, to thy teachers in the South, to thy wife and children in the West, to thy friends in the North, and regulate the zenith of thy religious relations above thee, and the nadir of thy servants below thee. Such is the religion thy father wants thee to have, and the performance of the ceremony shall remind thee of thy duties."

And Sigala looked up to the Blessed One with reverence as to his father and said: "Truly, Gotama, thou art the Buddha, the Blessed One, the holy teacher. I never knew what I was doing, but now I know. Thou hast revealed to me the truth that was hidden as one who bringeth a lamp into the darkness. I take my refuge in the Enlightened Teacher, in the truth that enlightens, and in the community of brethren who have been taught the truth."

Simha's Question Concerning Annihilation

AT that time many distinguished citizens were sitting together assembled in the town-hall and spoke in many ways in praise of the Buddha, of the Dharma, and of the Sangha. Simha, the general-in-chief, a disciple of the Niggantha sect, was sitting among them. And Simha thought: "Truly, the Blessed One must be the Buddha, the Holy One. I will go and visit him."

Then Simha, the general, went to the place where the Niggantha chief, Nataputta, was; and having approached him, he said: "I wish, Lord to visit the samana Gotama." Nataputta said: "Why should you, Simha, who believe in the result of actions according to their moral merit, go to visit the samana Gotama, who denies the result of actions? The samana Gotama, O Simha, denies the result of actions; he teaches the doctrine of non-action; and in this doctrine he trains his disciples."

Then the desire to go and visit the Blessed One, which had risen in Simha, the general, abated. Hearing again the praise of the Buddha, of the Dharma, and of the Sangha, Simha asked the Niggantha chief a second time; and again Nataputta persuaded him not to go.

When a third time the general heard some men of distinction extol the merits of the Buddha, the Dharma, and the Sangha, the general thought: "Truly the samana Gotama must be the Holy Buddha. What are the Nigganthas to me, whether they give their consent or not? I shall go without asking their permission to visit him, the Blessed One, the Holy Buddha." And Simha, the general, said to the Blessed One: "I have heard, Lord, that the samana Gotama denies the result of actions; he teaches the doctrine of non-action, saying that the actions of sentient beings do not receive their reward, for he teaches annihilation and the contemptibleness of all things; and in this doctrine he trains his disciples. Teachest thou the doing away of the soul and the burning away of man's being? Pray tell me, Lord, do those who speak thus say the truth, or do they bear false witness against the Blessed One, passing off a spurious Dharma as thy Dharma?"

The Blessed One said "There is a way, Simha, in which one who says so, is speaking truly of me; on the other hand, Simha, there is a way in which one who says the opposite is speaking truly of me, too. Listen, and I will tell thee: I teach, Simha, the not-doing of such actions as are unrighteous, either by deed, or by word, or by thought; I teach the not-bringing about of all those conditions of heart which are evil and not good. However, I teach, Simha, the doing of such actions as are righteous, by deed, by word, and by thought; I teach the bringing about of all those conditions of heart which are good and not evil.

"I teach, Simha, that all the conditions of heart which are evil and not good, unrighteous action by deed, by word, and by thought, must be burnt away. He who has freed himself, Simha, from all those conditions of heart which are evil and not good, he who has destroyed them as a palm-tree which is rooted out, so that they cannot grow up again, such a man has accomplished the eradication of self.

"I proclaim, Simha, the annihilation of egotism, of lust, of ill-will, of delusion. However, I do not proclaim the annihilation of forbearance, of love, of charity, and of truth. I deem, Simha, unrighteous actions contemptible, whether they be performed by deed, or by word, or by thought; but I deem virtue and righteousness praiseworthy."

Simha said: "One doubt still lurks in my mind concerning the doctrine of the Blessed One. Will the Blessed One consent to clear the cloud away so that I may understand the Dharma as the Blessed One teaches it?"

The Tathagata having given his consent, Simha continued: "I am a soldier, O Blessed One, and am appointed by the king to enforce his laws and to wage his wars. Does the Tathagata who teaches kindness without end and compassion with all sufferers, permit the punishment of the criminal? and further, does the Tathagata declare that it is wrong to go to war for the protection of our homes, our wives, our children, and our property? Does the Tathagata teach the doctrine of a complete self-surrender, so that I should suffer the evil-doer to do what he pleases and yield submissively to him who threatens to take by violence what is my own? Does the Tathagata maintain that all strife, including such warfare as is waged for a righteous cause should be forbidden?"

The Buddha replied: "He who deserves punishment must be punished, and he who is worthy of favour must be favoured. Yet at the same time he teaches to do no injury to any living being but to be full of love and kindness. These injunctions are not contradictory, for whosoever must be punished for the crimes which he has committed, suffers his injury not through the ill-will of the judge but on account of his evildoing. His own acts have brought upon him the injury that the executer of the law inflicts. When a magistrate punishes, let him not harbour hatred in his breast, yet a murderer, when put to death, should consider that this is the fruit of his own act. As soon as he will understand that the punishment will purify his soul, he will no longer lament his fate but rejoice at it."

The Blessed One continued: "The Tathagata teaches that all warfare in which man tries to slay his brother is lamentable, but he does not teach that those who go to war in a righteous cause after having exhausted all means to preserve the peace are blameworthy. He must be blamed who is the cause of war. The Tathagata teaches a complete surrender of self, but he does not teach a surrender of anything to those powers that are evil, be they men or gods or the elements of nature. Struggle must be, for all life is a struggle of some kind. But he that struggles should look to it lest he struggle in the interest of self against truth and righteousness.

"He who struggles in the interest of self, so that he himself may be great or powerful or rich or famous, will have no reward, but he who struggles for righteousness and truth, will have great reward, for even his defeat will be a victory. Self is not a fit vessel to receive any great success; self is small and brittle and its contents will soon be spilt for the benefit, and perhaps also for the curse, of others. Truth, however, is large enough to receive the yearnings and aspirations of all selves and when the selves break like soap-bubbles, their contents will be preserved and in the truth they will lead a life everlasting.

"He who goeth to battle, O Simha, even though it be in a righteous cause, must be prepared to be slain by his enemies, for that is the destiny of warriors; and should his fate overtake him he has no reason for complaint. But he who is victorious should remember the instability of earthly things. His success may be great, but be it ever so great the wheel of fortune may turn again and bring him down into the dust. However, if he moderates himself and, extinguishing all hatred in his heart lifts his down-trodden adversary up and says to him, Come now and make peace and let us be brothers, he will gain a victory that is not a transient success, for its fruits will remain forever. Great is a successful general, O Simha, but he who has conquered self is the greater victor.

"The doctrine of the conquest of self, O Simha, is not taught to destroy the souls of men, but to preserve them. He who has conquered self is more fit to live, to be successful, and to gain victories than he who is the slave of self. He whose mind is free from the illusion of self, will stand and not fall in that battle of life. He whose intentions are righteousness and justice, will meet with no failure, but be successful in his enterprises and his success will endure. He who harbours in his heart love of truth will live and not die, for he has drunk the water of immortality. Struggle then, O general, courageously; and fight thy battles vigorously, but be a soldier of truth and the Tathagata will bless thee."

When the Blessed One had spoken thus, Simha, the general, said: "Glorious Lord, glorious Lord! Thou hast revealed the truth. Great is the doctrine of the Blessed One. Thou, indeed, art the Buddha, the Tathagata, the Holy One. Thou art the teacher of mankind. Thou showest us the road of salvation, for this indeed is true deliverance. He who follows thee will not miss the light to enlighten his path. He will find blessedness and peace. I take my refuge, Lord, in the Blessed One, and in his doctrine, and in his brotherhood. May the Blessed One receive me from this day forth while my life lasts as a disciple who has taken refuge in him."

The Blessed One said: "Consider first, Simha, what thou doest. It is becoming that persons of rank like thyself should do nothing without due consideration."

Simha's faith in the Blessed One increased. He replied: "Had other teachers, Lord, succeeded in making me their disciple, they would carry around their banners through the whole city of Vesali, shouting: "Simha the general has become our disciple! For the second time, Lord, I take my refuge in the Blessed One, and in the Dharma, and in the Sangha; may the Blessed One receive me from this day forth while my life lasts as a disciple who has taken his refuge in him."

Said the Blessed One: "For a long time, Simha, offerings have been given to the Nigganthas in thy house. Thou shouldst therefore deem it right also in the future to give them food when they come to thee on their alms-pilgrimage." And Simha's heart was filled with joy. He said: "I have been told, Lord: 'The samana Gotama says: To me alone and to nobody else should gifts be given. My pupils alone and the pupils of no one else should receive offerings.' But the Blessed One exhorts me to give also to the Nigganthas. Well, Lord, we shall see what is seasonable. For the third time, Lord, I take my refuge in the Blessed One, and in his Dharma, and in his fraternity."

All Existence Is Spiritual

THERE was an officer among the retinue of Simha who had heard of the discourses of the Blessed One, and there was some doubt left in his heart. This man came to the Blessed One and said: "It is said, O Lord, that the samana Gotama denies the existence of the soul. Do they who say so speak the truth, or do they bear false witness against the Blessed One

And the Blessed One said: "There is a way in which those who say so are speaking truly of me; on the other hand, there is a way in which those who say so do not speak truly of me. The Tathagata teaches that there is no self. He who says that the soul is his self and that the self is the thinker of our thoughts and the actor of our deeds, teaches a wrong doctrine which leads to confusion and darkness. On the other hand, the Tathagata teaches that there is mind. He who understands by soul mind, and says that mind exists, teaches the truth which leads to clearness and enlightenment."

The officer said: "Does, then, the Tathagata maintain that two things exist? that which we perceive with our senses and that which is mental?"

Said the Blessed One: "I say to thee, thy mind is spiritual, but neither is the sense-perceived void of spirituality. The bodhi is eternal and it dominates all existence as the good law guiding all beings in their search for truth. It changes brute nature into mind, and there is no being that cannot be transformed into a vessel of truth."

The Lesson Given To Rahula

BEFORE Rahula, the son of Gotama Siddhattha and Yasodhara, attained to the enlightenment of true wisdom, his conduct was not always marked by a love of truth, and the Blessed One sent him to a distant vihara to govern his mind and to guard his tongue. After some time the Blessed One repaired to the place, and Rahula was filled with joy.

The Blessed One ordered the boy to bring him a basin of water and to wash his feet, and Rahula obeyed. When Rahula had washed the Tathagata's feet, the Blessed One asked: "Is the water now fit for drinking?"

"No, my Lord," replied the boy, "the water is defiled." Then the Blessed One said: "Now consider thine own case. Although thou art my son, and the grandchild of a king, although thou art a samana who has voluntarily given up everything, thou art unable to guard thy tongue from untruth, and thus defilest thou thy mind." And when the water had been poured away, the Blessed One asked again: "Is this vessel now fit for holding water to drink?"

"No, my Lord," replied Rahula, "the vessel, too, has become unclean." And the Blessed One said: "Now consider thine own case. Although thou wearest the yellow robe, art thou fit for any high purpose when thou hast become unclean like this vessel?" Then the Blessed One, lifting up the empty basin and whirling it round, asked: "Art thou not afraid lest it shall fall and break?" "No, my Lord," replied Rahula, it is cheap, its loss will not amount to much."

"Now consider thine own case," said the Blessed One. "Thou art whirled about in endless eddies of transmigration, and as thy body is made of the same substance as other material things that will crumble to dust, there is no loss if it be broken. He who is given to speaking untruths is an object of contempt to the wise."

Rahula was filled with shame, and the Blessed One addressed him once more: "Listen, and I will tell thee a parable: There was a king who had a very powerful elephant, able to cope with five hundred ordinary elephants. When going to war, the elephant was armed with sharp swords on his tusks, with scythes on his shoulders, spears on his feet, and an iron ball at his tail. The elephant-master rejoiced to see the noble creature so well equipped, and, knowing that a slight wound by an arrow in the trunk would be fatal, he had taught the elephant to keep his trunk well coiled up. But during the battle the elephant stretched forth his trunk to seize a sword. His master was frightened and consulted with the king, and they decided that the elephant was no longer fit to be used in battle.

"O Rahula! if men would only guard their tongues all would be well! Be like the fighting elephant who guards his trunk against the arrow that strikes in the centre. By love of truth the sincere escape iniquity. Like the elephant well subdued and quiet, who permits the king to mount on his trunk, thus the man that reveres righteousness will endure faithfully throughout his life." Rahula hearing these words was filled with deep sorrow; he never again gave any occasion for complaint, and forthwith he sanctified his life by earnest exertions.

The Sermon On Abuse

THE Blessed One observed the ways of society and noticed how much misery came from malignity and foolish offenses done only to gratify vanity and self-seeking pride. And the Buddha said: "If a man foolishly does me wrong, I will return to him the protection of my ungrudging love; the more evil comes from him, the more good shall go from me; the fragrance of goodness always comes to me, and the harmful air of evil goes to him."

A foolish man learning that the Buddha observed the principle of great love which commends the return of good for evil, came and abused him. The Buddha was silent, pitying his folly. When the man had finished his abuse, the Buddha asked him, saying: "Son, if a man declined to accept a present made to him, to whom would it belong?" And he answered: "In that case it would belong to the man who offered it."

"My son," said the Buddha "thou hast railed at me, but I decline to accept thy abuse, and request thee to keep it thyself. Will it not be a source of misery to thee? As the echo belongs to the sound, and the shadow to the substance, so misery will overtake the evil-doer without fail."

The abuser made no reply, and Buddha continued: "A wicked man who reproaches a virtuous one is like one who looks up and spits at heaven; the spittle soils not the heaven, but comes back and defiles his own person. The slanderer is like one who flings dust at another when the wind is contrary; the dust does but return on him who threw it. The virtuous man cannot be hurt and

the misery that the other would inflict comes back on himself."
The abuser went away ashamed, but he came again and took
refuge in the Buddha, the Dharma, and the Sangha.

The Buddha Replies To The Deva

ON a certain day when the Blessed One dwelt at Jetavana, the
garden of Anathapindika, a celestial deva came to him in the
shape of a Brahman whose countenance was bright and whose
garments were white like snow. The deva asked questions which
the Blessed One answered.

The deva said: "What is the sharpest sword? What is the
deadliest poison? What is the fiercest fire? What is the darkest
night?" The Blessed One replied: "A word spoken in wrath is the
sharpest sword; covetousness is the deadliest poison; passion is
the fiercest fire; ignorance is the darkest night."

The deva said: "Who gains the greatest benefit? Who loses
most? Which armour is invulnerable? What is the best weapon?"
The Blessed One replied: "He is the greatest gainer who to others,
and he loses most who greedily receives without gratitude.
Patience is an invulnerable armour; wisdom is the best weapon."

The deva said: "Who is the most dangerous thief? What is the
most precious treasure? Who is most successful in taking away by
violence not only on earth, but also in heaven? What is the
securest treasure-trove?" The Blessed One replied: "Evil thought is
the most dangerous thief; virtue is the most precious treasure. The
mind takes possession of everything not only on earth, but also in
heaven, and immortality is its securest treasure-trove."

The deva said: "What is attractive? What is disgusting? What is
the most horrible pain? What is the greatest enjoyment?" The
Blessed One replied: "Good is attractive; evil is disgusting. A bad
conscience is the most tormenting pain; deliverance is the height
of bliss."

The deva asked: "What causes ruin in the world? What breaks
off friendships? What is the most violent fever? Who is the best
physician?" The Blessed One replied: "Ignorance causes the ruin
of the world. Envy and selfishness break off friendships. Hatred is
the most violent fever, and the Buddha is the best physician."

The deva then asked and said: "Now I have only one doubt to
be solved; pray, clear it away: What is it fire can neither burn, nor
moisture corrode, nor wind crush down, but is able to reform the

whole world?" The Blessed One replied: "Blessing! Neither fire, nor moisture, nor wind can destroy the blessing of a good deed, and blessings reform the whole world."

The deva, having heard the words of the Blessed One, was full of exceeding joy. Clasping his hands, he bowed down before him in reverence, and disappeared suddenly from the presence of the Buddha.

Words Of Instruction

THE bhikkhus came to the Blessed One, and having saluted him with clasped hands they said: "O Master, thou all-seeing one, we all wish to learn; our ears are ready to hear, thou art our teacher, thou art incomparable. Cut off our doubt, inform us of the blessed Dharma, O thou of great understanding; speak in the midst of us, O thou who art all-seeing, as is the thousand-eyed Lord of the gods. We will ask the muni of great understanding, who has crossed the stream, gone to the other shore, is blessed and of a firm mind: How does a bhikkhu wander rightly in the world, after having gone out from his house and driven away desire?"

The Buddha said: "Let the bhikkhu subdue his passion for human and celestial pleasures, then, having conquered existence, he will command the Dhartna. Such a one will wander rightly in the world. He whose lusts have been destroyed, who is free from pride, who has overcome all the ways of passion, is subdued, perfectly happy, and of a firm mind. Such a one will wander rightly in the world. Faithful is he who is possessed of knowledge, seeing the way that leads to Nirvana; he who is not a partisan; he who is pure and virtuous, and has removed the veil from his eyes. Such a one will wander rightly in the world."

Said the bhikkhus: "Certainly, O Bhagavat, it is so: whichever bhikkhu lives in this way, subdued and having overcome all bonds, such a one will wander rightly in the world."

The Blessed One said: "Whatever is to be done by him who aspires to attain the tranquillity of Nirvana let him be able and upright, conscientious and gentle, and not proud. Let a man's pleasure be the Dharma, let him delight in the Dharma, let him stand fast in the Dharma, let him know how to inquire into the Dharma, let him not raise any dispute that pollutes the Dharma, and let him spend his time in pondering on the well-spoken truths of the Dharma.

"A treasure that is laid up in a deep pit profits nothing and may easily be lost. The real treasure that is laid up through charity and piety, temperance, self-control, or deeds of merit, is hid secure and cannot pass away. it is never gained by despoiling or wronging others, and no thief can steal it. A man, when he dies, must leave the fleeting wealth of the world, but this treasure of virtuous acts he takes with him. Let the wise do good deeds; they are a treasure that can never be lost."

Then the bhikkhus praised the wisdom of the Tathagata: "Thou hast passed beyond pain; thou art holy, O Enlightened One, we consider thee one that has destroyed his passions. Thou art glorious, thoughtful, and of great understanding. O thou who puttest an end to pain, thou hast carried us across our doubt. Because thou sawest our longing and carriedst us across our doubt, adoration be to thee, O muni, who hast attained the highest good in the ways of wisdom. The doubt we had before, thou hast cleared away, O thou clearly-seeing one; surely thou art a great thinker, perfectly enlightened, there is no obstacle for thee. All thy troubles are scattered and cut off; thou art calm, subdued, firm, truthful.

Adoration be to thee, O noble sage, adoration be to thee, O thou best of beings; in the world of men and gods there is none equal to thee. Thou art the Buddha, thou art the Master, thou art the muni that conquers Mara; after having cut off desire thou hast crossed over and carriest this generation to the other shore."

Amitabha, The Unbounded Light

ONE of the disciples came to the Blessed One with a trembling heart and his mind full of doubt. And he asked the Blessed One: "O Buddha, our Lord and Master, in what way do we give up the pleasures of the world, if thou forbiddest us to work miracles and to attain the supernatural? Is not Amitabha, the infinite light of revelation, the source of innumerable miracles?"

And the Blessed One, seeing the anxiety of a truth seeking mind, said: "O savaka, thou art a novice among the novices, and thou art swimming on the surface of samsara. How long will it take thee to grasp the truth? Thou hast not understood the words of the Tathagata. The law of karma is unbreakable, and supplications have no effect, for they are empty words."

Said the disciple: "Sayest thou there are no miraculous and wonderful things?"

The Blessed One replied: "Is it not a wonderful thing, mysterious and miraculous to the worldling, that a man who commits wrong can become a saint, that by attaining true enlightenment he will find the path of truth and abandon the evil ways of selfishness? The bhikkhu who renounces the transient pleasures of the world for the eternal bliss of holiness, performs the only miracle that can truly be called a miracle. A holy man changes the curses of karma into blessings. But the desire to perform miracles arises either from covetousness or from vanity. The mendicant does right who does not think: "People should salute me; who, though despised by the world, yet cherishes no ill-will towards it. That mendicant does right to whom omens, meteors, dreams, and signs are things abolished; he is free from all their evils. Amitabha, the unbounded light, is the source of wisdom, of virtue, of Buddhahood. The deeds of sorcerers and miracle-mongers are frauds, but what is more wondrous, more mysterious, more miraculous than Amitabha?"

"But, Master," continued the savaka, "Is the promise of the happy region vain talk and a myth?"

"What is this promise?" asked the Buddha; and the disciple replied: "There is in the west a paradise called the Pure Land, exquisitely adorned with gold and silver and precious gems. There are pure waters with golden sands, surrounded by pleasant walks and covered with large lotus flowers. Joyous music is heard, and flowers rain down three times a day. There are singing birds whose harmonious notes proclaim the praises of religion, and in the minds of those who listen to their sweet sounds, remembrance arises of the Buddha, the law, and the brotherhood. No evil birth is possible there, and even the name of hell is unknown. He who fervently and with a pious mind repeats the words 'Amitabha Buddha' will be transported to the happy region of this pure land, and when death draws nigh, the Buddha, with a company of saintly followers, will stand before him, and there will be perfect tranquillity."

"In truth," said the Buddha, "there is such a happy paradise. But the country is spiritual and it is accessible only to those that are spiritual. Thou sayest it lies in the west. This means, look for it where he who enlightens the world resides. The sun sinks down and leaves us in utter darkness, the shades of night steal over us, and Mara, the evil one, buries our bodies in the grave. Sunset is nevertheless no extinction, and where we imagine we see extinction, there is boundless light and inexhaustible life."

"I understand," said the savaka "that the story of the Western Paradise is not literally true."

"Thy description of paradise," the Buddha continued, "is beautiful; yet it is insufficient and does little justice to the glory of the pure land. The worldly can speak of it in a worldly way only; they use worldly similes and worldly words. But the pure land in which the pure live is more beautiful than thou canst say or imagine. However, the repetition of the name Amitabha Buddha is meritorious only if thou speak it with such a devout attitude of mind as will cleanse thy heart and attune thy will to do works of righteousness. He only can reach the happy land whose soul is filled with the infinite light of truth. He only can live and breathe in the spiritual atmosphere of the Western Paradise who has attained enlightenment. I say to thee, the Tathagata lives in the pure land of eternal bliss even now while he is still in the body. The Tathagata preaches the law of religion unto thee and unto the whole world, so that thou and thy brethren may attain the same peace, the same happiness."

Said the disciple: "Teach me, O Lord, the meditations to which I must devote myself in order to let my mind enter into the paradise of the pure land."

Buddha said: "There are five meditations. The first meditation is the meditation of love in which thou must so adjust thy heart that thou longest for the weal and welfare of all beings, including the happiness of thine enemies.

"The second meditation is the meditation of pity, in which thou thinkest of all beings in distress, vividly representing in thine imagination their sorrows and anxieties so as to arouse a deep compassion for them in thy soul.

"The third meditation is the meditation of joy in which thou thinkest of the prosperity of others and rejoicest with their rejoicings.

"The fourth meditation is the meditation on impurity, in which thou considerest the evil consequences of corruption, the effects of wrongs and evils. How trivial is often the pleasure of the moment and how fatal are its consequences!

"The fifth meditation is the meditation on serenity, in which thou risest above love and hate, tyranny and thraldom, wealth and want, and regardest thine own fate with impartial calmness and perfect tranquillity.

"A true follower of the Tathagata founds not his trust upon austerities or rituals, but giving up the idea of self relies with his whole heart upon Amitabha, which is the unbounded light of truth."

The Blessed One after having explained his doctrine of Amitabha, the immeasurable light which makes him who receives it a Buddha, looked into the heart of his disciple and saw still some doubts and anxieties. And the Blessed One said: "Ask me, my son, the questions which weigh upon thy soul."

The disciple said: "Can a humble monk, by sanctifying himself, acquire the talents of supernatural wisdom called Abhinnas and the supernatural powers called Iddhi? Show me the Iddhi-pada, the path to the highest wisdom. Open to me the Jhanas which are the means of acquiring samadhi, the fixity of mind which enraptures the soul. And the Blessed One said: "Which are the Abhinnas?"

The disciple replied: "There are six Abhinnas: The celestial eye; the celestial ear; the body at will or the power of transformation; the knowledge of the destiny of former dwellings, so as to know former states of existence; the faculty of reading the thoughts of others; and the knowledge of comprehending the finality of the stream of life."

And the Blessed One replied: "These are wondrous things; but verily, every man can attain them. Consider the abilities of thine own mind; thou wert born about two hundred leagues from here and canst thou not in thy thought, in an instant travel to thy native place and remember the details of thy father's home? Seest thou not with thy mind eye the roots of the tree which is shaken by the wind without being overthrown? Does not the collector of herbs see in his mental vision, whenever he pleases, any plant with its roots, its stern, its fruits, leaves, and even the uses to which it can be applied? Cannot the man who understands languages recall to his mind any word whenever he pleases, knowing its exact meaning and import? How much more does the Tathagata understand the nature of things; he looks into the hearts of men and reads their thoughts. He knows the evolution of beings and foresees their ends."

Said the disciple: "Then the Tathagata teaches that man can attain through the Jhanas the bliss of Abhinna." And the Blessed One asked in reply: "Which are the Jhanas through which man reaches Abhinna?"

The disciple replied: "There are four Jhanas. The first Jhana is seclusion in which one must free his mind from sensuality; the second Jhana is a tranquillity of mind full of joy and gladness; the third Jhana is a taking delight in things spiritual; the fourth Jhana is a state of perfect purity and peace in which the mind is above all gladness and grief."

"Good, my son," enjoined the Blessed One. "Be sober and abandon wrong practices which serve only to stultify the mind." Said the disciple: "Forbear with me, O Blessed One, for I have faith without understanding and I am seeking the truth. O Blessed One, O Tathagata, my Lord and Master, teach me the Iddhipada."

The Blessed One said: "There are four means by which Iddhi is acquired: Prevent bad qualities from arising. Put away bad qualities which have arisen. Produce goodness that does not yet exist. Increase goodness which already exists.-Search with sincerity, and persevere in the search. In the end thou wilt find the truth."

The Teacher Unknown

THE Blessed One said to Ananda: "There are various kinds of assemblies, O Ananda; assemblies of nobles, of Brahmans, of householders, of bhikkhus, and of other beings. When I used to enter an assembly, I always became, before I seated myself, in colour like unto the colour of my audience, and in voice like unto their voice. I spoke to them in their language and then with religious discourse I instructed, quickened, and gladdened them.

"My doctrine is like the ocean, having the same eight wonderful qualities. Both the ocean and my doctrine become gradually deeper. Both preserve their identity under all changes. Both cast out dead bodies upon the dry land. As the great rivers, when falling into the main, lose their names and are thenceforth reckoned as the great ocean, so all the castes, having renounced their lineage and entered the Sangha, become brethren and are reckoned the sons of Sakyamuni. The ocean is the goal of all streams and of the rain from the clouds, yet is it never overflowing and never emptied: so the Dharma is embraced by many millions of people, yet it neither increases nor decreases. As the great ocean has only one taste, the taste of salt, so my doctrine has only one flavour, the flavour of emancipation. Both the ocean and the Dharma are full of gems and pearls and jewels, and both afford a dwelling-place for mighty beings. These are the eight wonderful qualities in which my doctrine resembles the ocean.

"My doctrine is pure and it makes no discrimination between noble and ignoble, rich and poor. My doctrine is like unto water which cleanses all without distinction. My doctrine is like unto fire which consumes all things that exist between heaven and earth, great and small. My doctrine is like unto the heavens, for there is room in it, ample room for the reception of all, for men and women, boys and girls, the powerful and the lowly.

"But when I spoke, they knew me not and would say, 'Who may this be who thus speaks, a man or a god?' Then having instructed, quickened, and gladdened them with religious discourse, I would vanish away. But they knew me not, even when I vanished away."

Parables & Stories

THE Blessed One thought: "I have taught the truth which is excellent in the beginning, excellent in the middle, and excellent in the end; it is glorious in its spirit and glorious in its letter. But simple as it is, the people cannot understand it. I must speak to them in their own language. I must adapt my thoughts to their thoughts. They are like unto children, and love to hear tales. Therefore, I will tell them stories to explain the glory of the Dharma. If they cannot grasp the truth in the abstract arguments by which I have reached it, they may nevertheless come to understand it, if it is illustrated in parables."

The Man Born Blind

THERE was a man born blind, and he said: "I do not believe in the world of light and appearance. There are no colours, bright or sombre. There is no sun, no moon, no stars. No one has witnessed these things." His friends remonstrated with him, but he clung to his opinion: "What you say that you see," he objected, "are illusions. If colours existed I should be able to touch them. They have no substance and are not real. Everything real has weight, but I feel no weight where you see colours."

A physician was called to see the blind man. He mixed four simples, and when he applied them to the cataract of the blind man the gray film melted, and his eyes acquired the faculty of sight. The Tathagata is the physician, the cataract is the illusion of the thought "I am," and the four simples are the four noble truths.

The Lost Son

THERE was a householder's son who went away into a distant country, and while the father accumulated immeasurable riches, the son became miserably poor. And the son while searching for food and clothing happened to come to the country in which his father lived. The father saw him in his wretchedness, for he was ragged and brutalised by poverty, and ordered some of his servants to call him. When the son saw the place to which he was conducted, he thought, "I must have evoked the suspicion of a powerful man, and he will throw me into prison." Full of apprehension he made his escape before he had seen his father.

Then the father sent messengers out after his son, who was caught and brought back in spite of his cries and lamentations. Thereupon the father ordered his servants to deal tenderly with his son, and he appointed a labourer of his son's rank and education to employ the lad as a helpmate on the estate. And the son was pleased with his new situation. From the window of his palace the father watched the boy, and when he saw that he was honest and industrious, he promoted him higher and higher.

After some time, he summoned his son and called together all his servants, and made the secret known to them. Then the poor man was exceedingly glad and he was full of joy at meeting his father. Just so little by little, must the minds of men be trained for higher truths.

The Giddy Fish

THERE was a bhikkhu who had great difficulty in keeping his senses and passions under control; so, resolving to leave the Order, he came to the Blessed One to ask him for a release from the vows. And the Blessed One said to the bhikkhu: "Take heed, my son, lest thou fall a prey to the passions of thy misguided heart. For I see that in former existences, thou hast suffered much from the evil consequences of lust, and unless thou learnest to conquer thy sensual desire, thou wilt in this life be ruined through thy folly.

"Listen to a story of another existence of thine, as a fish. The fish could be seen swimming lustily in the river, playing with his mate. She, moving in front, suddenly perceived the meshes of a net, and slipping around escaped the danger; but he, blinded by love, shot eagerly after her and fell straight into the mouth of the net. The fisherman pulled the net up, and the fish, who complained bitterly of his sad fate, saying, 'this indeed is the bitter fruit of my folly,' would surely have died if the Bodhisattva had not chanced to come by, and, understanding the language of the fish, took pity on him. He bought the poor creature and said to him: 'My good fish, had I not caught sight of thee this day, thou wouldst have lost thy life. I shall save thee, but henceforth avoid the evil of lust.' With these words he threw the fish into the water.

"Make the best of the time of grace that is offered to thee in thy present existence, and fear the dart of passion which, if thou guard not thy senses, will lead thee to destruction."

Four Kinds Of Merit

THERE was a rich man who used to invite all the Brahmans of the neighbourhood to his house, and, giving them rich gifts, offered great sacrifices to the gods.

But the Blessed One said: "If a man each month repeat a thousand sacrifices and give offerings without ceasing, he is not equal to him who but for one moment fixes his mind upon righteousness." The Buddha continued: "There are four kinds of offering: first, when the gifts are large and the merit small; secondly, when the gifts are small and the merit small; thirdly, when the gifts are small and the merit large; and fourthly, when the gifts are large and the merit is also large.

"The first is the case of the deluded man who takes away life for the purpose of sacrificing to the gods, accompanied by carousing and feasting. Here the gifts are great, but the merit is small indeed. Next, the gifts are small and the merit is also small, when from covetousness and an evil heart a man keeps to himself a part of that which he intends to offer.

"The merit is great, however, while the gift is small, when a man makes his offering from love and with a desire to grow in wisdom and in kindness. And lastly, the gift is large and the merit is large, when a wealthy man, in an unselfish spirit and with the wisdom of a Buddha, gives donations and founds institutions for the best of mankind to enlighten the minds of his fellow-men and to administer unto their needs."

The Light Of The World

THERE was a certain Brahman in Kosambi, a wrangler and well versed in the Vedas. As he found no one whom he regarded his equal in debate he used to carry a lighted torch in his hand, and when asked for the reason of his strange conduct, he replied: 'The world is so dark that I carry this torch to light it up, as far as I can." A samana sitting in the market-place heard these words and said: "My friend, if thine eyes are blind to the sight of the omnipresent light of the day, do not call the world dark. Thy torch adds nothing to the glory of the sun and thy intention to illumine the minds of others is as futile as it is arrogant." Whereupon the Brahman asked: "Where is the sun of which thou speakest?" And the samana replied: "The wisdom of the Tathagata is the sun of the mind. His radiancy is glorious by day and night, and he whose faith is strong will not lack light on the path to Nirvana where he will inherit bliss everlasting."

Luxurious Living

WHILE the Buddha was preaching his doctrine for the conversion of the world in the neighbourhood of Savatthi, a man of great wealth who suffered from many ailments came to him with clasped hands and said: "World-honoured Buddha, pardon me for my want of respect in not saluting thee as I ought but I suffer greatly from obesity, excessive drowsiness, and other complaints, so that I cannot move without pain."

The Tathagata, seeing the luxuries with which the man was surrounded asked him: "Hast thou a desire to know the cause of thy ailments?" And when the wealthy man expressed his willingness to learn, the Blessed One said: "There are five things which produce the condition of which thou complainest: opulent dinners, love of sleep, hankering after pleasure, thoughtlessness, and lack of occupation. Exercise self-control at thy meals, and take upon thyself some duties that will exercise thy abilities and make thee useful to thy fellow-men. In following this advice thou wilt prolong thy life."

The rich man remembered the words of the Buddha and after some time having recovered his lightness of body and youthful buoyancy returned to the World-honoured One and, coming afoot without horses and attendants, said to him: "Master, thou hast cured my bodily ailments; I come now to seek enlightenment of my mind."

And the Blessed One said: "The worldling nourishes his body, but the wise man nourishes his mind. He who indulges in the satisfaction of his appetites works his own destruction; but he who walks in the path will have both the salvation from evil and a prolongation of life.

The Sower

BHARADVAJA, a wealthy Brahman farmer, was celebrating his harvest-thanksgiving when the Blessed One came with his alms-bowl, begging for food. Some of the people paid him reverence, but the Brahman was angry and said: "O samana, it would be more fitting for thee to go to work than to beg. I plough and sow, and having ploughed and sown, I eat. If thou didst likewise, thou, too, wouldst have something to eat."

The Tathagata answered him and said: "O Brahman, I too, plough and sow, and having ploughed and sown, I eat." "Dost thou profess to be a husbandman?" replied the Brahman. "Where, then, are thy bullocks? Where is the seed and the plough?"

The Blessed One said: "Faith is the seed I sow: good works are the rain that fertilises it; wisdom and modesty are the plough; my mind is the guiding-rein; I lay hold of the handle of the law; earnestness is the goad I use, and exertion is my draught-ox. This ploughing is ploughed to destroy the weeds of illusion. The harvest it yields is the immortal fruits of Nirvana, and thus all sorrow ends." Then the Brahman poured rice-milk into a golden bowl and offered it to the Blessed One, saying: "Let the Teacher of mankind partake of the rice-milk, for the venerable Gotama ploughs a ploughing that bears the fruit of immortality."

The Outcast

WHEN Bhagavat dwelt at Savatthi in the Jetavana, he went out with his alms-bowl to beg for food and approached the house of a Brahman priest while the fire of an offering was blazing upon the altar. And the priest said: "Stay there, O shaveling; stay there, O wretched samana; thou art an outcast."

The Blessed One replied: "Who is an outcast? An outcast is the man who is angry and bears hatred; the man who is wicked and hypocritical, he who embraces error and is full of deceit. Whosoever is a provoker and is avaricious, has evil desires, is envious, wicked, shameless, and without fear to commit wrong, let him be known as an outcast. Not by birth does one become an outcast, not by birth does one become a Brahman; by deeds one becomes an outcast, by deeds one becomes a Brahman.

The Peacemaker

IT is reported that two kingdoms were on the verge of war for the possession of a certain embankment which was disputed by them. And the Buddha seeing the kings and their armies ready to fight, requested them to tell him the cause of their quarrels. Having heard the complaints on both sides, he said:

"I understand that the embankment has value for some of your people; has it any intrinsic value aside from its service to your men?"

"It has no intrinsic value whatever" was the reply.

The Tathagata continued: "Now when you go to battle is it not sure that many of your men will be slain and that you yourselves, O kings, are liable to lose your lives?" And they said: "It is sure that many will be slain and our own lives be jeopardised."

"The blood of men, however," said Buddha, "has it less intrinsic value than a mound of earth?" "No," the kings said, "The lives of men and above all the lives of kings, are priceless." Then the Tathagata concluded: care you going to stake that which is priceless against that which has no intrinsic value whatever—The wrath of the two monarchs abated, and they came to a peaceable agreement.

In Search Of A Thief

HAVING sent out his disciples, the Blessed One himself wandered from place to place until he reached Uruvela. On his way he sat down in a grove to rest, and it happened that in that same grove was a party of thirty friends who were enjoying themselves with their wives; and while they were sporting, some of their goods were stolen. Then the whole party went in search of the thief and, meeting the Blessed One sitting under a tree, saluted him and said: "Pray, Lord, didst thou see the thief pass by with our goods?"

And the Blessed One said: "Which is better for you, that you go in search for the thief or for yourselves?" And the youths cried: "In search for ourselves!"

"Well then," said the Blessed One "sit down and I will preach the truth to you." And the whole party sat down and they listened eagerly to the words of the Blessed One. Having grasped the truth, they praised the doctrine and took refuge in the Buddha.

Walking On Water

SOUTH of Savatthi is a great river, on the banks of which lay a hamlet of five hundred houses. Thinking of the salvation of the people, the World-honoured One resolved to go to the village and preach the doctrine. Having come to the riverside he sat down beneath a tree, and the villagers seeing the glory of his appearance approached him with reverence; but when he began to preach, they believed him not.

When the world-honoured Buddha had left Savatthi Sariputta felt a desire to see the Lord and to hear him preach. Coming to the river where the water was deep and the current strong, he said to himself: "This stream shall not prevent me. I shall go and see the Blessed One," and he stepped upon the water which was as firm under his feet as a slab of granite. When he arrived at a place in the middle of the stream where the waves were high, Sariputta's heart gave way, and he began to sink. But rousing his faith and renewing his mental effort, he proceeded as before and reached the other bank.

The people of the village were astonished to see Sariputta, and they asked how he could cross the stream where there was neither a bridge nor a ferry. Sariputta replied: "I lived in ignorance until I heard the voice of the Buddha. As I was anxious to hear the doctrine of salvation, I crossed the river and I walked over its troubled waters because I had faith. Faith. nothing else, enabled me to do so, and now I am here in the bliss of the Master's presence."

The World-honoured One added: "Sariputta, thou hast spoken well. Faith like thine alone can save the world from the yawning gulf of migration and enable men to walk dryshod to the other shore." And the Blessed One urged to the villagers the necessity of ever advancing in the conquest of sorrow and of casting off all shackles so as to cross the river of worldliness and attain deliverance from death. Hearing the words of the Tathagata, the villagers were filled with joy and believing in the doctrines of the Blessed One embraced the five rules and took refuge in his name.

The Last Days

WHEN the Blessed One was residing on the mountain called Vulture's Peak, near Rajagaha, Ajatasattu king of Magadha, who reigned in the place of Bimbisara, planned an attack on the Vajjis, and he said to Vassakara, his prime minister: "I will root out the Vajjis, mighty though they be. I will destroy the Vajjis; I will bring them to utter ruin! Come now, O Brahman, and go to the Blessed One; inquire in my name for his health, and tell him my purpose. Bear carefully in mind what the Blessed One may say, and repeat it to me, for the Buddhas speak nothing untrue."

When Vassakara, the prime minister, had greeted the Blessed One and delivered his message, the venerable Ananda stood behind the Blessed One and fanned him, and the Blessed One said to him: "Hast thou heard, Ananda, that the Vajjis hold full and frequent public assemblies?" He replied, "Lord, so I have heard."

"So long, Ananda," said the Blessed One, "as the Vajjis hold these full and frequent public assemblies, they may be expected not to decline, but to prosper. So long as they meet together in concord, so long as they honour their elders, so long as they respect womanhood, so long as they remain religious, performing all proper rites, so long as they extend the rightful protection, defence and support to the holy ones, the Vajjis may be expected not to decline, but to prosper." Then the Blessed One addressed Vassakara and said: "When I stayed, O Brahman, at Vesali, I taught the Vajjis these conditions of welfare, that so long as they should remain well instructed, so long as they will continue in the right path, so long as they live up to the precepts of righteousness, we could expect them not to decline, but to prosper."

As soon as the king's messenger had gone, the Blessed One had the brethren, that were in the neighbourhood of Rajagaha, assembled in the service-hall and addressed them, saying: "I will teach you, O bhikkhus, the conditions of the welfare of a community. Listen well, and I will speak.

"So long, O bhikkhus, as the brethren hold full and frequent assemblies, meeting in concord, rising in concord, and attending in concord to the affairs of the Sangha; so long as they, O bhikkhus, do not abrogate that which experience has proved to be good, and introduce nothing except such things as have been carefully tested; so long as their elders practice justice; so long as the brethren esteem, revere, and support their elders, and hearken unto their words; so long as the brethren are not under the influence of craving, but delight in the blessings of religion, so that good and holy men shall come to them and dwell among them in quiet; so long as the brethren shall not be addicted to sloth and idleness; so long as the brethren shall exercise themselves in the sevenfold higher wisdom of mental activity, search after truth, energy, joy, modesty, self-control, earnest contemplation, and equanimity of mind, so long the Sangha may be expected to prosper. Therefore, O bhikkhus, be full of faith, modest in heart, afraid of sin, anxious to learn, strong in energy, active in mind, and full of wisdom."

Sariputta's Faith

THE Blessed One proceeded with a great company of the brethren to Nalanda; and there he stayed in a mango grove. Now the venerable Sariputta came to the place where the Blessed One was, and having saluted him, took his seat respectfully at his side, and said: "Lord! such faith have I in the Blessed One, that methinks there never has been, nor will there be, nor is there now any other, who is greater or wiser than the Blessed One, that is to say, as regards the higher wisdom."

Replied the Blessed One: "Grand and bold are the words of thy mouth, Sariputta: verily, thou hast burst forth into a song of ecstasy! Surely then thou hast known all the Blessed Ones who in the long ages of the past have been holy Buddhas?" "Not so, O Lord!" said Sariputta.

And the Lord continued: "Then thou hast perceived all the Blessed Ones who in the long ages of the future shall be holy Buddhas?" "Not so, O Lord!"

"But at least then, O Sariputta, thou knowest me as the holy Buddha now alive, and hast penetrated my mind." "Not even that, O Lord!"

"Thou seest then, Sariputta, that thou knowest not the hearts of the holy Buddhas of the past nor the hearts of those of the future. Why, therefore, are thy words so grand and bold? Why burstest thou forth into such a song of ecstasy?"

"O Lord! I have not the knowledge of the hearts of all the Buddhas that have been and are to come, and now are. I only know the lineage of the faith. Just as a king, Lord, might have a border city, strong in its foundations, strong in its ramparts and with one gate only; and the king might have a watchman there, clever, expert, and wise, to stop all strangers and admit only friends. And on going over the approaches all about the city, he might not be able so to observe all the joints and crevices in the ramparts of that city as to know where such a small creature as a cat could get out. That might well be. Yet all living beings of larger size that entered or left the city, would have to pass through that gate. Thus only is it, Lord, that I know the lineage of the faith. I know that the holy Buddhas of the past, putting away all lust, ill-will, sloth, pride, and doubt, knowing all those mental faults which make men weak, training their minds in the four kinds of mental activity, thoroughly exercising themselves in the sevenfold higher wisdom, received the full fruition of Enlightenment. And I know that the holy Buddhas of the times to come will do the same. And I know that the Blessed One, the holy Buddha of today, has done so now."

"Great is thy faith, O Sariputta," replied the Blessed One, "but take heed that it be well grounded."

The Visit To Pataliputta

WHEN the Blessed One had stayed as long as convenient at Nalanda, he went to Pataliputta, the frontier town of Magadha; and when the disciples at Pataliputta heard of his arrival, they invited him to their village rest-house. And the Blessed One robed himself, took his bowl and went with the brethren to the rest-house. There he washed his feet, entered the hall, and seated himself against the centre pillar, with his face towards the east. The brethren, also, having washed their feet, entered the hall, and took their seats round the Blessed One, against the western wall, facing the east. And the lay devotees of Pataliputta, having also washed their feet, entered the hall, and took their seats opposite the Blessed One against the eastern wall, facing towards the west.

Then the Blessed One addressed the lay-disciples of Pataliputta, and he said: "Fivefold O householders, is the loss of the wrong-doer through his want of rectitude. In the first place, the wrong-doer, devoid of rectitude, falls into great poverty through sloth; in the next place, his evil repute gets noised abroad; thirdly, whatever society he enters, whether of Brahmans, nobles, heads of houses, or samanas, he enters shyly and confusedly; fourthly, he is full of anxiety when he dies; and lastly, on the dissolution of the body after death, his mind remains in an unhappy state. Wherever his karma continues, there will be suffering and woe. This, O householders, is fivefold loss of the evil-doer!

"Fivefold, O householders, is the gain of the well-doer through his practice of rectitude. In the first place the well doer, strong in rectitude, acquires property through his industry; in the next place, good reports of him are spread abroad; thirdly, whatever society he enters, whether of nobles, Brahmans, heads of houses, or members of the order, he enters with confidence and self-possession; fourthly, he dies without anxiety; and, lastly, on the dissolution of the body after death, his mind remains in a happy state. Wherever his karma continues, there will be heavenly bliss and peace. This, O householders, is the fivefold gain of the well doer." When the Blessed One had taught the disciples, and incited them, and roused them, and gladdened them far into the night with religious edification, he dismissed them, saying, "The night is far spent, O householders. It is time for you to do what ye deem most fit."

"Be it so, Lord!" answered the disciples of Pataliputta, and rising from their seats, they bowed to the Blessed One, and keeping him on their right hand as they passed him, they departed thence.

While the Blessed One stayed at Pataliputta, the king of Magadha sent a messenger to the governor of Pataliputta to raise fortifications for the security of the town. The Blessed One seeing the labourers at work predicted the future greatness of the place, saying: "The men who build the fortress act as if they had consulted higher powers. For this city of Pataliputta will be a dwelling-place of busy men and a centre for the exchange of all kinds of goods. But three dangers hang over Pataliputta, that of fire, that of water, that of dissension."

When the governor heard of the prophecy of Pataliputta's future, he greatly rejoiced and named the city-gate through which the Buddha had gone towards the river Ganges, "The Gotama Gate." Meanwhile the people living on the banks of the Ganges arrived in great numbers to pay reverence to the Lord of the world; and many persons asked him to do them the honour to cross over in their boats. But the Blessed One considering the number of the boats and their beauty did not want to show any partiality, and by accepting the invitation of one to offend all the others. He therefore crossed the river without any boat, signifying thereby that the rafts of asceticism and the gaudy gondolas of religious ceremonies were not staunch enough to weather the storms of samsara, while the Tathagata can walk dry-shod over the ocean of worldliness. And as the city gate was called after the name of the

Tathagata so the people called this passage of the river "Gotama Ford."

The Buddha's Farewell

WHEN the Blessed One had remained as long as he wished at Ambapali's grove, he went to Beluva, near Vesali. There the Blessed One addressed the brethren, and said: "O mendicants, take up your abode for the rainy season round about Vesali, each one according to the place where his friends and near companions may live. I shall enter upon the rainy season here at Beluva."

When the Blessed One had thus entered upon the rainy season there fell upon him a dire sickness and sharp pains came upon him even unto death. But the Blessed One, mindful and self-possessed, bore his ailments without complaint. Then this thought occurred to the Blessed. "It would not be right for me to pass away from life without addressing the disciples, without taking leave of the order. Let me now, by a strong effort of the will, subdue this sickness, and keep my hold on life till the allotted time has come." And the Blessed One by a strong effort of the will subdued the sickness, and kept his hold on life till the time he fixed upon should come. And the sickness abated.

Thus the Blessed One began to recover; and when he had quite got rid of the sickness, he went out from the monastery, and sat down on a seat spread out in the open air. And the venerable Ananda, accompanied by many other disciples, approached where the Blessed One was, saluted him, and taking a seat respectfully on one side, said: "I have beheld, Lord, how the Blessed One was in health, and I have beheld how the Blessed One had to suffer. And though at the sight of the sickness of the Blessed One my body became weak as a creeper, and the horizon became dim to me, and my faculties were no longer clear, yet notwithstanding I took some little comfort from the thought that the Blessed One would not pass away from existence until at least he had left instructions as touching the order."

The Blessed One addressed Ananda on behalf of the order, saying: "What, then, Ananda, does the order expect of me? I have preached the truth without making any distinction between doctrine hidden or revealed; for in respect of the truth, Ananda, the Tathagata has no such thing as the closed fist of a teacher, who keeps some things back.

"Surely, Ananda, should there be any one who harbour the thought, 'It is I who will lead the brotherhood,' or, 'The order is dependent upon me,' he should lay down instructions in any matter concerning the order. Now the Tathagata, Ananda, thinks not that it is he who should lead the brotherhood, or that the order is dependent upon him. Why, then, should the Tathagata leave instructions in any matter concerning the order?

"I am now grown old, O Ananda, and full of years; my journey is drawing to its close, I have reached the sum of my days, I am turning eighty years of age. Just as a wornout cart can not be made to move along without much difficulty, so the body of the Tathagata can only be kept going with much additional care. It is only when the Tathagata, Ananda, ceasing to attend to any outward thing, becomes plunged in that devout meditation of heart which is concerned with no bodily object, it is only then that the body of the Tathagata is at ease.

"Therefore, O Ananda, be ye lamps unto yourselves. Rely on yourselves, and do not rely on external help. Hold fast to the truth as a lamp. Seek salvation alone in the truth. Look not for assistance to any one besides yourselves.

"And how, Ananda, can a brother be a lamp unto himself, rely on himself only and not on any external help, holding fast to the truth as his lamp and seeking salvation in the truth alone, looking not for assistance to any one besides himself? Herein, O Ananda, let a brother, as he dwells in the body, so regard the body that he, being strenuous, thoughtful, and mindful, may, whilst in the world, overcome the grief which arises from the body's cravings. While subject to sensations let him continue so to regard the sensations that he, being strenuous, thoughtful, and mindful, may, whilst in the world, overcome the grief which arises from the sensations. And so, also, when he thinks or reasons, or feels, let him so regard his thoughts that being strenuous, thoughtful and mindful he may, whilst in the world, overcome the grief which arises from the craving due to ideas, or to reasoning, or to feeling.

"Those who, either now or after I am dead, shall be lamps unto themselves, relying upon themselves only and not relying upon any external help, but holding fast to the truth as their lamp, and seeking their salvation in the truth alone, and shall not look for assistance to any one besides themselves, it is they, Ananda, among my bhikkhus, who shall reach the very topmost height! But they must be anxious to learn."

The Buddha Announces His Death

SAID the Tathagata to Ananda: "In former years, Ananda, Mara, the Evil One, approached the holy Buddha three times to tempt him. And now, Ananda, Mara, the Evil One, came again today to the place where I was, and, standing beside me, addressed me in the same words as he did when I was resting under the shepherd's Nigrodha tree on the bank of the Neranjara River: 'Be greeted, thou Holy One. Thou hast attained the highest bliss and it is time for thee to enter into the final Nirvana.' — And when Mara had thus spoken, Ananda, I answered him and said: 'Make thyself happy, O wicked one; the final extinction of the Tathagata shall take place before long.'"

The venerable Ananda addressed the Blessed One and said: "Vouchsafe, Lord, to remain with us, O Blessed One I for the good and the happiness of the great multitudes, out of pity for the world, for the good and the gain of mankind!" Said the Blessed One: "Enough now, Ananda, beseech not the Tathagata!"

And again, a second time, the venerable Ananda besought the Blessed One in the same words. He received from the Blessed One the same reply. And again, the third time, the venerable Ananda besought the Blessed One to live longer; and the Blessed One said: "Hast thou faith, Ananda?" Said Ananda: "I have, my Lord!"

The Blessed One, seeing the quivering eyelids of Ananda, read the deep grief in the heart of his beloved disciple, and he asked again: "Hast thou, indeed, faith, Ananda?" And Ananda said: "I have faith, my Lord."

Then the Blessed One continued: "If thou hast faith, Ananda in the wisdom of the Tathagata, why, then, Ananda, dost thou trouble the Tathagata even until the third time? Have I not formerly declared to you that it is in the very nature of all compound things that they must be dissolved again? We must separate ourselves from all things near and dear to us, and must leave them. How then, Ananda, can it be possible for me to remain, since everything that is born, or brought into being, and organised, contains within itself the inherent necessity of dissolution? How, then, can it be possible that this body of mine should not be dissolved? No such condition can exist! And this mortal existence, O Ananda, has been relinquished, cast away, renounced, rejected, and abandoned by the Tathagata."

And the Blessed One said to Ananda: "Go now, Ananda, and

assemble in the Service Hall such of the brethren as reside in the neighbourhood of Vesali."

Then the Blessed One proceeded to the Service Hall, and sat down there on the mat spread out for him. And when he was seated, the Blessed One addressed the brethren, and said: "O brethren, ye to whom the truth has been made known, having thoroughly made yourselves masters of it, practise it, meditate upon it, and spread it abroad, in order that pure religion may last long and be perpetuated, in order that it may continue for the good and happiness of the great multitudes, out of pity for the world, and to the good and gain of all living beings! Star-gazing and astrology, forecasting lucky or unfortunate events by signs, prognosticating good or evil, all these are things forbidden. He who lets his heart go loose without restraint shall not attain Nirvana; therefore, must we hold the heart in check, and retire from worldly excitements and seek tranquillity of mind. Eat your food to satisfy your hunger, and drink to satisfy your thirst. Satisfy the necessities of life like the butterfly that sips the flower, without destroying its fragrance or its texture. It is through not understanding and grasping the four truths, O brethren, that we have gone astray so long and wandered in this weary path of transmigrations, both you and I, until we have found the truth. Practise the earnest meditations I have taught you. Continue in the great struggle against sin. Walk steadily in the roads of saintship. Be strong in moral powers. Let the organs of your spiritual sense be quick. When the seven kinds of wisdom enlighten your mind, you will find the noble, eightfold path that leads to Nirvana.

"Behold, O brethren, the final extinction of the Tathagata will take place before long. I now exhort you, saying: All component things must grow old and be dissolved again. Seek ye for that which is permanent, and work out your salvation with diligence."

Chunda, The Smith

THE Blessed One went to Pava. When Chunda, the worker in metals, heard that the Blessed One had come to Pava and was staying in his mango grove, he came to the Buddha and respectfully invited him and the brethren to take their meal at his house. And Chunda prepared rice-cakes and a dish of dried boar's meat.

When the Blessed One had eaten the food prepared by Chunda, the worker in metals, there fell upon him a dire sickness, and sharp pain came upon him even unto death. But the Blessed One, mindful and self-possessed, bore it without complaint. And the Blessed One addressed the venerable Ananda, and said: "Come, Ananda, let us go on to Kusinara."

On his way the Blessed One grew tired, and he went aside from the road to rest at the foot of a tree, and said: "Fold the robe, I pray thee, Ananda, and spread it out for me. I am weary, Ananda, and must rest awhile!" "Be it so, Lord!" said the venerable Ananda; and he spread out the robe folded fourfold. The Blessed One seated himself, and when he was seated he addressed the venerable Ananda, and said: "Fetch me some water, I pray thee, Ananda. I am thirsty, Ananda, and would drink."

When he had thus spoken, the venerable Ananda said to the Blessed One: "But just now, Lord, five hundred carts have gone across the brook and have stirred the water; but a river, O Lord, is not far off. Its water is clear and pleasant, cool and transparent, and it is easy to get down to it. the Blessed One may both drink water and cool his limbs."

A second time the Blessed One addressed the venerable Ananda, saying: "Fetch me some water, I pray thee, Ananda, I am thirsty, Ananda, and would drink."

And a second time the venerable Ananda said: "Let us go to the river."

Then the third time the Blessed One addressed the venerable Ananda, and said: "Fetch me some water, I pray thee, Ananda, I am thirsty, Ananda and would drink." "Be it so, Lord!" said the venerable Ananda in assent to the Blessed One; and, taking a bowl, he went down to the streamlet. And lo! the streamlet, which, stirred up by wheels, had become muddy, when the venerable Ananda came up to it, flowed clear and bright and free from all turbidity. And he thought: "How wonderful, how marvellous is the great might and power of the Tathagata!"

Ananda brought the water in the bowl to the Lord, saying: "Let the Blessed One take the bowl. Let the Happy One drink the water. Let the Teacher of men and gods quench his thirst. Then the Blessed One drank of the water."

Now, at that time a man of low caste, named Pukkusa, a young Malla, a disciple of Alara Kalama, was passing along the high road from Kusinara to Pava. Pukkusa, the young Malla, saw the Blessed

One seated at the foot of a tree. On seeing him he went up to the place where the Blessed One was, and when he had come there, he saluted the Blessed One and took his seat respectfully on one side. Then the Blessed One instructed, edified, and gladdened Kukkusa, the young Malla, with religious discourse.

Aroused and gladdened by the words of the Blessed One, Pukkusa, the young Malla, addressed a certain man who happened to pass by, and said: "Fetch me, I pray thee, my good man, two robes of cloth of gold, burnished and ready for wear."

"Be it so, sir!" said that man in assent to Pukkusa, the young Malla; and he brought two robes of cloth of gold, burnished and ready for wear.

The Malla Pukkusa presented the two robes of cloth of gold, burnished and ready for wear, to the Blessed One, saying: "Lord, these two robes of burnished cloth of gold are ready for wear. May the Blessed One show me favour and accept them at my hands!"

The Blessed One said: "Pukkusa, robe me in one, and Ananda in the other one." And the Tathagata's body appeared shining like a flame, and he was beautiful above all expression.

The venerable Ananda said to the Blessed One: "How wonderful a thing is it, Lord, and how marvellous, that the colour of the skin of the Blessed One should be so clear, so exceedingly bright! When I placed this robe of burnished cloth of gold on the body of the Blessed One, lo! it seemed as if it had lost its splendour!"

The Blessed One said: "There are two occasions on which a Tathagata's appearance becomes clear and exceeding bright. In the night, Ananda, in which a Tathagata attains to the supreme and perfect insight, and in the night in which he passes finally away in that utter passing away which leaves nothing whatever of his earthly existence to remain."

And the Blessed One addressed the venerable Ananda, and said: "Now it may happen, Ananda, that some one should stir up remorse in Chunda, the smith, by saying: 'It is evil to thee, Chunda, and loss to thee, that the Tathagata died, having eaten his last meal from thy provision.' Any such remorse, Ananda, in Chunda, the smith, should be checked by saying: 'It is good to thee, Chunda, and gain to thee, that the Tathagata died, having eaten his last meal from thy provision.' From the very mouth of the Blessed One, O Chunda, have I heard, from his own mouth have I received this saying, "These two offerings of food are of equal fruit and of much greater profit than any other: the offerings of food which a Tathagata accepts when he has attained perfect enlightenment and when he passes away by the utter passing away in which nothing whatever of his earthly existence remains behind these two offerings of food are of equal fruit and of equal profit, and of much greater fruit and much greater profit than any other. There has been laid up by Chunda, the smith, a karma redounding to length of life, redounding to good birth, redounding to good fortune, redounding to good fame, redounding to the inheritance of heaven and of great power. In this way, Ananda, should be checked any remorse in Chunda, the smith."

Then the Blessed One, perceiving that death was near, uttered these words: "He who gives away shall have real gain. He who subdues himself shall be free, he shall cease to be a slave of passions. The righteous man casts off evil; and by rooting out lust, bitterness, and illusion, do we reach Nirvana."

Metteyya

THE Blessed One proceeded with a great company of the brethren to the sala grove of the Mallas, the Upavattana of Kusinara on the further side of the river Hirannavati, and when he had arrived he addressed the venerable Ananda, and said: "Make ready for me, I pray you, Ananda, the couch with its head to the north, between the twin sala trees. I am weary, Ananda, and wish to lie down."

"Be it so, Lord!" said the venerable Ananda, and he spread a couch with its head to the north, between the twin sala trees. And the Blessed One laid himself down, and he was mindful and self-possessed.

Now, at that time the twin sala trees were full of bloom with flowers out of season; and heavenly songs came wafted from the skies, out of reverence for the successor of the Buddhas of old. And Ananda was filled with wonder that the Blessed One was thus honoured. But the Blessed One said: "Not by such events, Ananda, is the Tathagata rightly honoured, held sacred, or revered. But the devout man, who continually fulfils the greater and lesser duties, walking according to the precepts, it is who rightly honours, holds sacred, and reveres the Tathagata with the worthiest homage. Therefore, O Ananda, be ye constant in the fulfillment of the greater and of the lesser duties, and walk according to the precepts; thus, Ananda, will ye honour the Master."

Then the venerable Ananda went into the vihara, and stood leaning against the doorpost, weeping at the thought: "Alas! I remain still but a learner, one who has yet to work out his own perfection. And the Master is about to pass away from me—who is so kind!"

Now, the Blessed One called the brethren, and said: "Where, O brethren, is Ananda?" One of the brethren went and called Ananda. And Ananda came and said to the Blessed One: "Deep darkness reigned for want of wisdom; the world of sentient creatures was groping for want of light; then the Tathagata lit up the lamp of wisdom, and now it will be extinguished again, ere he has brought it out."

The Blessed One said to the venerable Ananda, as he sat there by his side: "Enough, Ananda Let not thy self be troubled; do not weep! Have I not already, on former occasions, told you that it is in the very nature of all things most near and dear unto us that we must separate from them and leave them? The foolish man conceives the idea of 'self,' the wise man sees there is no ground on which to build the idea of 'self,' thus he has a right conception of the world and well concludes that all compounds amassed by sorrow will be dissolved again, but the truth will remain. Why should I preserve this body of flesh, when the body of the excellent law will endure? I am resolved; having accomplished my purpose and attended to the work set me, I look for rest I For a long time, Ananda, thou hast been very near to me by thoughts and acts of such love as is beyond all measure. Thou hast done well, Ananda I Be earnest in effort and thou too shalt soon be free from evils, from sensuality, from selfishness, from delusion, and from ignorance!"

Ananda, suppressing his tears, said to the Blessed One: "Who shall teach us when thou art gone?"

And the Blessed One replied: "I am not the first Buddha who came upon earth, nor shall I be the last. In due time another Buddha will arise in the world, a Holy One, a supremely enlightened One, endowed with wisdom in conduct, auspicious, knowing the universe, an incomparable leader of men, a master of angels and mortals. He will reveal to you the same eternal truths which I have taught you. He will preach his religion, glorious in its origin, glorious at the climax, and glorious at the goal, in the spirit and in the letter. He will proclaim a religious life, wholly perfect and pure; such as I now proclaim."

Ananda said: "How shall we know him?" The Blessed One said: "He will be known as Metteyya, which means 'he whose name is kindness.'"

Entering Into Nirvana

THEN the Mallas, with their young men and maidens and their wives, being grieved, and sad, and afflicted at heart, went to the Upavattana, the sala grove of the Mallas, and wanted to see the Blessed One, in order to partake of the bliss that devolves upon those who are in the presence of the Holy One.

The Blessed One addressed them and said: "Seeking the way, ye must exert yourselves and strive with diligence. It is not enough to have seen me Walk as I have commanded you; free yourselves from the tangled net of sorrow. Walk in the path with steadfast aim. A sick man may be cured by the healing power of medicine and will be rid of all his ailments without beholding the physician. He who does not do what I command sees me in vain. This brings no profit; while he who lives far off from where I am and yet walks righteously is ever near me. A man may dwell beside me, and yet, being disobedient, be far away from me. Yet he who obeys the Dharma will always enjoy the bliss of the Tathagata's presence."

Then the mendicant Subhadda went to the sala grove of the Mallas and said to the venerable Ananda: "I have heard from fellow mendicants of mine, who were deep stricken in years and teachers of great experience: 'Sometimes and full seldom do Tathagatas appear in the world, the holy Buddhas.' Now it is said that today in the last watch of the night, the final passing away of the samana Gotama will take place. My mind is full of uncertainty, yet have I faith in the samana Gotama and trust he will be able so to present the truth that I may become rid of my doubts. O that I might be allowed to see the Samana Gotama!"

When he had thus spoken the venerable Ananda said to the mendicant Subhadda: "Enough! friend Subhadda. Trouble not the Tathagata. The Blessed One is weary." Now the Blessed One overheard this conversation of the venerable Ananda with the mendicant Subhadda. And the Blessed One called the venerable Ananda, and said: "Ananda! Do not keep out Subhadda. Subhadda may be allowed to see the Tathagata. Whatever Subhadda will ask of me, he will ask from a desire for knowledge, and not to annoy me, and whatever I may say in answer to his questions, that he will quickly understand."

Then the venerable Ananda said: "Step in, friend Subhadda; for the Blessed One gives thee leave."

When the Blessed One had instructed Subhadda, and aroused and gladdened him with words of wisdom and comfort, Subhadda said to the Blessed One: "Glorious Lord, glorious Lord! Most excellent are the words of thy mouth, most excellent! They set up that which has been overturned, they reveal that which has been hidden. They point out the right road to the wanderer who has gone astray. They bring a lamp into the darkness so that those who have eyes to see can see. Thus, Lord, the truth has been made known to me by the Blessed One and I take my refuge in the Blessed One, in the Truth, and in the Order. May the Blessed One accept me as a disciple and true believer, from this day forth as long as life endures."

And Subhadda, the mendicant, said to the venerable Ananda: "Great is thy gain, friend Ananda, great is thy good fortune, that for so many years thou hast been sprinkled with the sprinkling of discipleship in this brotherhood at the hands of the Master himself!"

Now the Blessed One addressed the venerable Ananda, and said: "It may be, Ananda, that in some of you the thought may arise, 'The word of the Master is ended, we have no teacher more!' But it is not thus, Ananda, that you should regard it. It is true that no more shall I receive a body, for all future sorrow has now forever passed away. But though this body will be dissolved, the Tathagata remains. The truth and the rules of the order which I have set forth and laid down for you all, let them, after I am gone, be a teacher unto you.When I am gone, Ananda, let the order, if it should so wish, abolish all the lesser and minor precepts."

Then the Blessed One addressed the brethren, and said: "There may be some doubt or misgiving in the mind of a brother as to the Buddha, or the truth, or the path. Do not have to reproach yourselves afterwards with the thought, 'We did not inquire of the Blessed One when we were face to face with him.' Therefore inquire now, O brethren, inquire freely."

The brethren remained silent. Then the venerable Ananda said to the Blessed One: "Verily, I believe that in this whole assembly of the brethren there is not one brother who has any doubt or misgiving as to the Buddha, or the truth, or the path!"

Said the Blessed One: "It is out of the fullness of faith that thou hast spoken, Ananda! But Ananda, the Tathagata knows for certain that in this whole assembly of the brethren there is not one brother who has any doubt or misgiving as to the Buddha, or the truth, or the path! For even the most backward, Ananda, of all these brethren has become converted, and is assured of final salvation."

Then the Blessed One addressed the brethren and said: "If ye now know the Dharma the cause of all suffering, and the path of salvation, O disciples, will ye then say: 'We respect the Master, and out of reverence for the Master do we thus speak?'" The brethren replied: "That we shall not, O Lord."

And the Holy One continued: "Of those beings who live in ignorance, shut up and confined, as it were, in an egg, I have first broken the egg-shell of ignorance and alone in the universe obtained the most exalted, universal Buddhahood. Thus, O disciples, I am the eldest, the noblest of beings.

"But what ye speak, O disciples, is it not even that which ye have yourselves known, yourselves seen, yourselves realised?" Ananda and the brethren said: "It is, O Lord."

Once more the Blessed One began to speak: "Behold now, brethren," said he, "I exhort you, saying, 'Decay is inherent in all component things, but the truth will remain forever Work out your salvation with diligence!" This was the last word of the Tathagata. Then the Tathagata fell into a deep meditation, and having passed through the four jhanas, entered Nirvana.

When the Blessed One entered Nirvana there arose, at his passing out of existence, a mighty earthquake, terrible and awe-inspiring: and the thunders of heaven burst forth, and of those of the brethren who were not yet free from passions some stretched out their arms and wept, and some fell headlong on the ground, in anguish at the thought: "Too soon has the Blessed One died! Too soon has the Happy One passed away from existence! Too soon has the Light of the world gone out!"

Then the venerable Anuruddha exhorted the brethren and said: "Enough, my brethren! Weep not, neither lament! Has not the Blessed One formerly declared this to us, that it is in the very nature of all things near and dear unto us, that we must separate from them and leave them, since everything that is born, brought into being, and organised, contains within itself the inherent necessity of dissolution? How then can it be possible that the body of the Tathagata should not be dissolved? No such condition can exist! Those who are free from passion will bear the loss, calm and self-possessed, mindful of the truth he has taught us."

The venerable Anuruddha and the venerable Ananda spent the rest of the night in religious discourse. Then the venerable Anuruddha said to the venerable Ananda: "Go now, brother Ananda, and inform the Mallas of Kusinara saying, 'The Blessed One has passed away: do, then, whatsoever seemeth fit!'" And when the Mallas had heard this saying they were grieved, and sad, and afflicted at heart.

Then the Mallas of Kusinara gave orders to their attendants, saying, "Gather together perfumes and garlands, and all the music in Kusinara!" And the Mallas of Kusinara took the perfumes and garlands, and all the musical instruments, and five hundred garments, and went to the sala grove where the body of the Blessed One lay. There they passed the day in paying honour and reverence to the remains of the Blessed One, with hymns, and music, and with garlands and perfumes, and in making canopies of their garments, and preparing decorative wreaths to hang thereon. And they burned the remains of the Blessed One as they would do to the body of a king of kings.

When the funeral pyre was lit, the sun and moon withdrew their shining, the peaceful streams on every side were torrent-swollen, the earth quaked, and the sturdy forests shook like aspen leaves, whilst flowers and leaves fell untimely to the ground, like scattered rain, so that all Kusinara became strewn knee-deep with mandara flowers raining down from heaven.

When the burning ceremonies were over, Devaputta said to the multitudes that were assembled round the pyre: "Behold, O brethren, the earthly remains of the Blessed One have been dissolved, but the truth which he has taught us lives in our minds and cleanses us from all error. Let us, then, go out into the world, as compassionate and merciful as our great master, and preach to all living beings the four noble truths and the eightfold path of righteousness, so that all mankind may attain to a final salvation, taking refuge in the Buddha, the Dharma, and the Sangha."

When the Blessed One had entered into Nirvana and the Mallas had burned the body with such ceremonies as would indicate that he was the great king of kings, ambassadors came from all the empires that at the time had embraced his doctrine, to claim a share of the relics; and the relics were divided into eight parts and eight dagobas were erected for their preservation. One dagoba was erected by the Mallas, and seven others by the seven kings of those countries whose people had taken refuge in the Buddha.

Conclusion

WHEN the Blessed One had passed away into Nirvana, the disciples came together and consulted what to do in order to keep the Dharma pure and uncorrupted by heresies.

Upali rose, saying: "Our great Master used to say to the brethren: 'O bhikkhus! after my final entrance into Nirvana you must reverence and obey the law. Regard the law as your master. The law is like unto a light that shines in the darkness, pointing out the way; it is also like unto a precious jewel to gain which you must shun no trouble, and be ready to bring any sacrifice; even, should it be needed, your own lives. Obey the Dharma which I have revealed to you; follow it carefully and if as in no way different from myself.' Such were the words of the Blessed One. The law, accordingly, which the Buddha has left us as a precious inheritance has now become the visible body of the Tathagata. Let us, therefore, revere it and keep it sacred. For what is the use of erecting dagobas for relics, if we neglect the spirit of the Master's teachings?"

Then Anuruddha arose and said: "Let us bear in mind, O brethren, that Gotama Siddhattha has revealed the truth to us. He was the Holy One and the Perfect One and the Blessed One, because the eternal truth had taken abode in him. The Tathagata taught us that the truth existed before he was born into this world, and will exist after he has entered into Nirvana. The Tathagata said: 'The truth is omnipresent and eternal, endowed with excellencies innumerable, above all human nature, and ineffable in its holiness.'

"Now let us bear in mind that not this or that law which is revealed to us in the Dhanna is the Buddha, but the entire truth, the truth which is eternal, omnipresent, immutable, and most excellent. Many regulations of the Sangha are temporary; they were prescribed because they suited the occasion and were needed for some transient emergency. The truth, however, is not temporary. The truth is not arbitrary nor a matter of opinion, but can be investigated, and he who earnestly searches for the truth will find it. The truth is hidden to the blind, but he who has the mental eye sees the truth. The truth is Buddha's essence, and the truth will remain the ultimate standard. Let us, then, revere the truth; let us inquire into the truth and state it, and let us obey the truth. For the truth is Buddha our Master, our Teacher."

And Kassapa rose and said: "Truly thou hast spoken well, O brother Anuruddha. Neither is there any conflict of opinion on the meaning of our religion. For the Blessed One possesses three personalities and each of them is of equal importance to us. There is the Dharma Kaya. There is the Nirmana Kaya. There is the Sambhoga Kaya. Buddha is the all-excellent truth, eternal, omnipresent, and immutable: this is the Sambhoga Kaya which is in a state of perfect bliss. Buddha is the all-loving teacher assuming the shape of the beings whom he teaches: this is the Nirmana Kaya, his apparitional body. Buddha is the all-blessed dispensation of religion; he is the spirit of the Sangha and the meaning of the commands left us in his sacred word, the Dharma: this is the Dharma Kaya, the body of the most excellent law.

"If Buddha had not appeared to us as Gotama Sakyamuni, how could we have the sacred traditions of his doctrine? And if the generations to come did not have the sacred traditions preserved in the Sangha, how could they know anything of the great Sakyamuni? And neither we nor others would know anything about the most excellent truth which is eternal, omnipresent, and immutable. Let us then keep sacred and revere the traditions; let us keep sacred the memory of Gotama Sakyamuni, so that people may find the truth."

Then the brethren decided to convene a synod to lay down the doctrines of the Blessed One, to collate the sacred writings, and to establish a canon which should serve as a source of instruction for future generations.